The Outlaw
{or}
Farewell, Old West

NICHOLAS CLAPP

SUNBELT PUBLICATIONS, INC.

SAN DIEGO, CALIFORNIA

The Outlaw's Violin: Farewell, Old West

Sunbelt Publications, Inc.
Copyright © 2019 by Nicholas Clapp
All rights reserved. First edition 2019

Cover and book design by Barry Age
Cover illustration by Rebecca Kriz
Project management by Deborah Young
Printed in United States of America

Sunbelt Publications, Inc.
P.O. Box 191126
San Diego, CA 92159-1126
(619) 258-4911, fax: (619) 258-4916
www.sunbeltpublications.com

22 21 20 19   4 3 2 1

Library of Congress Cataloging-in-Publication Data
Names: Clapp, Nicholas, author.
Title: The outlaw's violin, or, Farewell, old West / Nicholas Clapp.
Other titles: Farewell, old West
Description: San Diego, CA : Sunbelt Publications, Inc., [2019]
Identifiers: LCCN 2018046488 | ISBN 9781941384497 (softcover : alk. paper)
Subjects: LCSH: Fraser, Billy, (William Henry), 1880-1954. | Outlaws–West
  (U.S.)–Biography. | Violinists–West (U.S.)–Biography. | West
  (U.S.)–Biography. | West (U.S.)–History–1890-1945.
Classification: LCC F595.F84 C55 2019 | DDC 978/.03092 [B] –dc23 LC record
available at https://lccn.loc.gov/2018046488

For Bonnie

CONTENTS

For well over a hundred years, an Old West handcrafted violin has survived – before turning up in a Mojave Desert swap meet, bashed and battered. But since then, restored and playable.

Inked doggerel and drawings decorate the violin, and chronicle the life and times of its creator and owner, prospector-miner-musician Billy Fraser.

As a young man, he was to proclaim himself the "Montana Kid," and then – better and badder – he was to become the "Montana Outlaw."

Storm, California's Mojave Desert.

Prologue

Churned by raging winds, summer storm clouds broke the grasp of California's Sierra Nevada Range, to shroud and darken the Mojave Desert to the east. Lightning blazed; thunder ripped the sky. And below and by night, a sole kerosene lamp flickered in the window of a crumbling adobe, a forlorn remnant of a settlement that once fancied itself "Ophir City."

Rain washed the dust-encrusted window to reveal, inside, a figure hunched over a table, surrounded by scattered artifacts of a mine's workshop. A grease-crusted pile of gears, a broken air pump, a haphazard pile of sledges and drilling steels.

Here then was Billy Fraser, as he neared his thirtieth birthday. As a miner and prospector, he'd seen a lot, and experienced his share of good times and bad. He was presently adding finishing touches and adjustments to a homemade violin crafted from scrap lumber, and featuring as a sound box, a round, hollowed-out coyote melon.[1]

Tentatively, he drew a bow across the strings, and cringed. A dreadful sound! But ah, he'd neglected to soften his bow with rosin.

Another pass with the bow, and that was more like it. The tone was on the squeaky side, but what could he expect? With an alacrity that surprised him, Fraser sawed a verse of "The Miner's Song," a gold-seeker's classic. He half sang, half hummed:

> Broad ledges, rich in hidden gold,
>> Lie temptingly before us.
> We need no Midas' magic wand,
>> Nor wizard rod divining;
> The pickaxe, spade and brawny hand
>> Are sorcerers in mining.

A peal of thunder accented the ditty.

In a clutter of junk that he'd swept from his worktable, Billy recalled a rusty pen and an India ink bottle. Its contents, alas, were cracked and crusty. But then – how could he escape it? – all about, soaking him head to toe, there was dripping, even cascading water. The night's storm raged on. He filled the bottle, shook it, then shook it some more. The water blackened. He dipped the pen, seized his newly crafted violin, and on the flank of its coyote melon gourd, inscribed:

---

[1] Why the name "coyote melon"? The answer dates to 1868, when by foot, a botanist crossed the Sierra Nevadas to where "the plants of the desert were all new to him and excited his intense interest." There, he was to discover and describe *Cucurbita palmata*, a cousin of the pumpkin. Seeking a common name, he noted nearby coyote scat flecked with the plant's seeds and immediately deduced who ate what, thus the name. Botanist Sereno Watson, it would appear, was a kindred soul to Billy Fraser, his pursuit plants and flowers as opposed to gold and silver. "The reserve which lasted through his life left him all the more free to prosecute his chosen work without the distraction of society. But his reserve was not that of a misanthrope." He was a loner, a good-hearted loner. And the gourd he named over the years provided bowls to Indians, soap to early white settlers, and soon, solace to a lonely prospector. (Quotes from Watson's obituary in the *American Journal of Science,* vol. XLII)

§ **Detail, the violin's gourd.**

What was happening here?

Was this fellow, benign as he created a violin, actually an outlaw? And what about the *Montana* part, seeing as the locale was in California's Mojave Desert?

The answer could have been that no other state in the Far West boasted – or feared – as many gun-toting, cold-blooded outlaws as Montana. Indeed, well into the 1900s, the very word *Montana* conjured a state of mind, and not a good one. It plagued sheriffs and terrified townsfolk – and on the flip side of the coin, *it appealed to wayward souls bent by a need to be someone.*

As an outlaw, to be feared, and in a craven way, respected.

In any case, Billy, the fellow in a desert ruin would – in coming hours, or perhaps days or months, there's no way to tell – decorate his violin with doggerel and images of his life and times. The instrument would mirror his high hopes, record his wistful laments, and be a window into his shifting state of mind.

A San Francisco's wharf in the waning days of the Gold Rush.
The *Esmeralda* was similar to the ship in the center distance.

Just Wrap Me Up & Throw Me Away

The three-masted sloop *Esmeralda* tacked to starboard, then back to port, to dock at a San Francisco wharf at the end of an arduous journey. Sturdy and slow, she had been built with Arctic exploration in mind, but with the advent of iron-hulled ships, had been relegated to life as a tramp, restlessly roaming the seas. Her hold was currently laden with massive pumps to further western America's ever-deepening quest for gold and silver, a quest daunted by sustained and often scalding bursts of underground water. The *Esmeralda's* recent run had departed Glasgow, called at Cornwall, taken on provisions in New York, then rounded the Horn. There'd been passengers picked up and dropped off, with only a single family weathering the entire three-month run. They were the Frasers: father Donald, his wife Hattie, their daughter Mary, and an infant son Alexander – with another on the way.

A ship's hawser had barely been cast as the Frasers scrambled to disembark the *Esmeralda*, and for good reason. Crying, nay wailing, mother Hattie was in labor, and would be lucky to make it to a doctor.

She didn't.

And little Billy, formally to become William Henry Fraser, came into the world howling on the salt-bleached planks of a San Francisco wharf. Up by the mizzenmast, the *Esmeralda's* captain confided to his first mate, "At last, riddance is ours." He then called out, "Yon Frasers, good luck to you all! (this laced with sarcasm, the captain being a Campbell, a clan ill-disposed toward Frasers.)

What happened next can only be surmised. The Frasers may have sought the help of a midwife or doctor, and they would have sought a place to stay, likely a back room in a second-rate boarding house. By now on their American adventure, they would have been low on coin. On their voyage they would have looked after their own food, with the *Esmeralda's* captain providing only water. And they weren't that well off to begin with.

But at least they were on solid ground, prompting father Donald to seek employment as a miner, or better yet, a pump man, his calling back in Scotland. Accordingly, he could have made inquiries at a saloon or, better yet gossip-wise, spied the red-striped pole of a barber shop.

The news therein was not encouraging. In the three months his family had been at sea, the California Gold Rush had pretty much run its course, with any mines still operating sufficiently staffed. A year or so earlier, he could have signed at the mighty Empire in Grass Valley, with its 11,000 foot incline shaft, 500 miles of tunnels, and lakes of underground water to be pumped out. But this was not to be. Rather, he was advised to try his luck in Virginia City, off in Nevada. A few years earlier they'd discovered the "Big Bonanza," the most recent of several great globs of silver and gold. And surely, there'd soon be another, probably deeper, in a zone of spouting and surging water, just the thing for a master pump man.

There was a spring in Donald's step as he returned to his family's humble accommodation. Employment was at hand, and amazingly only a day away if they took the Virginia and Truckee's *Lightning Express*. Yes, tickets were expensive, all but wiping out their remaining funds, but leaving in the late afternoon, they'd overnight arrive in what had been proclaimed "the richest place on earth." Young Mary and Alexander were all for it. Was Hattie, new with child, up to it? It really didn't matter. Donald had the tickets in hand.

Meanwhile, by lantern light, down by the docks, the *Esmeralda's* captain was signing up passengers for a return run to New York. As there was little prospective cargo, he called them "paying ballast." And a week hence, he would indifferently write in his log,

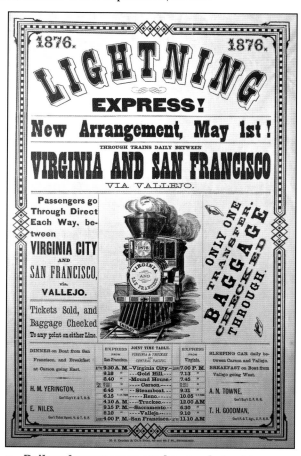

♪ **Railroads were promoted as roads to riches.**

Squally – N.W. by W. At breakfast time a woman from the
Old Country, a Mrs. Thomas died. Left three children.
At eventide sails were furled and ship hove-to while
funeral lasted. Wasted an hour. At 5 o'clock the body of
her whose spirit had gone to glory was consigned to the
great deep wrapped in canvas with two bags of ballast.

And below deck, a sallow, work-worn fellow was to write,
"Here I find every man's hand against neighbor, and even
friend, if anything is to be got thereby. Every man serves his
own end even when to the disadvantage of others." They were
a sour lot: captain, crew – and passengers, who a dozen years
ago had pursued the West's golden dream, with now, hardly a
whit to show for it.

At the same time, crossing California's Sierra Nevadas, the
Frasers (fitful baby Billy excepted) marveled at the glory of
snow-capped, moonlit peaks. They plunged through tunnels
and timbered snow sheds. As dawn stole across the desert,
they pulled into Reno, and transferred to a narrow-gauge
Virginia & Truckee train that would haul them up a mountain
rich in silver and gold. Their ticket to glory!

In time for breakfast (not that they could afford breakfast),
they set foot in Virginia City.

There was a dusting of snow on the ground, and the air
was clear and crisp – bracing – yet almost immediately Donald
sensed something. Something eerily wrong. As most all miners
in his homeland, he'd read accounts of Virginia's streets teem-
ing with fortune seekers, be they miners or moguls. Where
were they? He led his family up the hill to C Street, the main
street. They peered in the windows of shops and saloons, and

saw little activity beyond an occasional barkeep polishing a glass. Sure, it was first thing in the morning, but shouldn't the circus that was Virginia City be performing around the clock? No constables in sight, no drunks even. And what did he hear – or rather, not hear? What about clanging mine bells signaling men and descending or ore rising, or the racket of thundering round-the-clock stamp mills?

He hoped he was wrong but it would appear that Virginia City's world was running down. In *borrasca*, barren times, and on a slide to oblivion.

The Frasers would have continued on to B Street, and a view of the city's smokestacks.

A few were puffing away, but not that many. Donald took refuge, if not comfort in the fact that he could well be on the ground floor of a new bonanza, a deeper bonanza, and accordingly in need of knowledgeable pump men, the likes of him.

Hattie reminded him: she, the baby, they all needed somewhere to stay. Tonight. And to their relief, this wasn't a problem. Most every street offered forsaken homes, with inquiry eliciting variations on, "They've gone. Fled. Take your pick."

The Frasers settled in, and by evening had cleaned up a place, scavenged scrap wood for a fire, and shared cans of beef and beans, purchased with the very last of their coin.

The next morning, Donald would have made the rounds of mines belching steam and smoke, only to be dismissed not by words, but by baleful shakes of heads. By noon, a dozen of them. Didn't give up, though. Skipping lunch, he had a go at the Union, a consolidation of a dozen hapless mines.

At dusk, Virginia City and the Consolidated Virginia Mine, with 1,200 feet underground, a vast cavern, the site of the city's renowned – and now exhausted – "Big Bonanza."

"You're Cornish?"

Donald wasn't, but who was to know. "Good guess," he said.[2]

"Your cap. Could tell by your cap. And your experience?"

"A pump man."

"Ah, a pump man." And tilting back in his swivel chair, whoever it was queried, "How about big pumps? Not donkey engines. *Really big* pumps."

"Any and all pumps."

[2] While Donald was Scottish, his wife Hattie was Cornish – close enough.

"One with a 100 ton flywheel and a 2,500 foot, 300 ton pump rod?"

Donald's eyes widened. If a pump man had a dream, this was it! He steadied himself. "Then I'm your man."

Be that as it may, like many – if not all – things in life, there was a hitch. The fellow pulling the night shift, an old timer, had given notice, and would be returning to his village back in England at the end of the month. In the meantime, would Fraser settle for cutting a winze on the 1,400 foot level? "Pay is $4.00 a day, despite bad times. As at present."

As elated as a Scotsman can get, Donald might well have stopped by a Scots-run bakery on his way to his new home, and asking in Gaelic, bought a dozen pasties on credit. They'd suffice for dinner.

The next morning, he answered the call of the Union's whistle, and set about sinking a winze, an incline from one level down to the next. The rock was hard; the work was hard. With a hand drill and a sledge hammer, sink half a dozen or more holes, pack them with Giant Powder and fuses, light same, shout "Fire in the hole!" and walk, not run to the 1,400 foot station. Run and you could trip, and that could be final.

As promised, a month later the nighttime custody of the Union Mine's great pump was Donald's. And with it a stretch of gainful employment. From time to time there was talk of shutting the pump down, but there was ever a ray of hope – that any day they could encounter a deeper-than-anything-before bonanza.

Though not a Fraser, the fellow in the picture wears a
Cornish cap, and labors by the light of a single candle set in a
spiked Cornish holder.

Months, then years went by and the Frasers had a life in
a dying town. A good, if not prosperous life. They dined out,
once at the grand International Hotel. They attended plays at
Piper's Opera House, and particularly enjoyed a production of
Hamlet in which in the interest of authenticity, Cornish miners
had dug a "practical" grave. Gravedigger actors shoveled real

ore up onto the stage, and when Hamlet and Laertes jumped into Ophelia's grave, they barked their shins on real bedrock.

Turning seven, son Alexander landed a job – the best that a kid could expect, delivering sharpened steel to pockets of miners, and carting off their thunder jugs. And little brother Billy was enrolled as a scholar in the Fourth Ward School – but then, for no particular reason, he ran away from home. On his birthday, his parents had afforded him a new, velvet suit. And topped with his best cap, and with ten cents tied up in a handkerchief, he bravely set out for the town of Gold Hill, a mile distant. A heavy rain had preceded his departure, and although the sun was now shining, he encountered a pond of ocean-like proportions before he had gone a block. He tried to ford it, slipped, and fell. Between mud and water, his suit gained pounds in weight, and when with the assistance of a neighbor he had scrambled out of the pond on the side nearest home, he had no heart for continuing on.

On Billy's return, his father Donald, awakened from a morning snooze after a graveyard shift tending the Union's giant pump, brimmed with wrath as only a riled Scotsman can. He grumbled in his native Gaelic, then railed in English, "I work hard, buy your now ruined suit, and this is what I get for it?"

"I just felt like it, I guess…" Billy mumbled. Which set off a further tirade, punctuated with repeated exclamations of the word "Wayward!"

Billy hung his head, did his best to appear contrite. Even so, he felt an appeal – to the word "Wayward!" If that's what I am, then why not? That's what I'll be.

This was but the first of his misadventures. With a comment of "untoward pugnacity," he was bounced from the Fourth Ward School. For pennies an hour, he was relegated to separate a mine dump's pay dirt from dead ore.

The boys' older sister didn't fare all that well. Witness a letter from a one-time suitor:

> Dear Mary – You will have to hunt for another chap, for
> I have married Martha Brown. She is not as good-looking
> as yourself, but she has heaps of money and we have
> gone to housekeeping in good shape. So good-bye. – Alf.

On her part, mother Hattie was struck by how richly and extravagantly women dressed in Virginia City. Proficient at sewing, she took up swathing them in silk, and as Donald smirked, bedecking them in flower gardens hats. She did well, charging as much as $80 for a dress, and then taking a mildly malign delight in, through her parlor window, watching the ample skirts of her creations mop up mud and tobacco juice splattered on the walkway fronting their little house.

Not that she was ill disposed as to Virginians and their city. Quite the contrary, she successfully campaigned to establish a soup house for the poor. She rented an abandoned cart shop for $15 a month, and solicited cold victuals from restaurants and wilted vegetables from grocers. Soon, the project was feeding five hundred people three times a day. She expected the tide of poor and broken men and women to diminish in a month or so, but it didn't. After dinner, the three women running the place, seeking subscriptions to stay open, walked so far and so fast that their feet blistered; they then had trouble sleeping before rising to prepare breakfast at five in the morning.

Worn and exhausted, they closed their soup house. And Hattie, not in the best of health, was never to recover.

Methodist Donald grumped as Virginia's Catholic Sisters of Mercy offered her a bed at their St. Mary's Hospital, where sadly, she died, whether by the scourge of cholera, pox, or by a broken heart.

Harkening to this sad day, the coyote melon gourd of Billy Fraser's violin (yet to be crafted) appears to have been at some point bashed in. Only a "From This –" and a "Mother's Kiss" remained legible.

Whatever the full inscription, it had a plaintive air of a son's love for his mother, heightened as she faded away.

The city – the Frasers, everyone – was overtaken by a pervasive gloom, and a fear that dispossessed, "done in" miners could plunder and might even torch Virginia City. They were resentful, given to rage, reckless.

Though not Donald, a Cornishman at the controls of the Union's pump.

Grim headlines tumbled one after another: **THE SAVAGE MINE NEARLY AS HOT AS HADES, A FALL OF ONE THOUSAND THREE HUNDRED FEET,** and **THE FATAL BLUNDER.** Cages were lowered and raised with such dizzying speed that a moment of carelessness could sever a leg, arm or head. Jets of boiling water burned faces and hands; Giant powder was accidently ignited. A letter to the *Territorial Enterprise* openly questioned the grace of God when a runaway ore car took out miner Richard Pearce, on Sunday a preacher at a local Methodist chapel.

Nevertheless, all the while, father Donald tended his pump, until the day when the order came, from capitalists in San Francisco or back East, no one was sure, to extract the pillars of ore left in place to prop open the Union's Mine's maze of working.

There was a term for this, succinct and brutal: "To put out the eyes of the mine."

After a last shift of miners took out pillars rich in silver and gold, then "climbed to the grass," Donald Fraser shut down the Union's mighty pump.

The mine's workings, foot by foot, level by level, flooded.

As he partook a frugal dinner with his father and brother, Billy – bereft, lightly stoked with self-esteem – might well have exclaimed, "Just wrap me up and throw me away."

And indeed, near all of Virginia City could have echoed his sentiment: "Just wrap us up and throw us away."

From the pages of the *Virginia Evening Chronicle*, Donald read aloud:

> A miner always takes his life in hands when he takes
> his dinner-bucket and starts for the mines, for he does
> not know whether he will return alive... Underground,
> there is a sense of horrible confinement, from which
> there appears no escape, and in which there must be
> a constant struggle to keep from falling exhausted...
> The suffering of intense heat is every-day life to a miner.[3]

Time for the Frasers to move on.

But where to?

---

[3] Quoted in Mary McNair Matthews, *Ten Years in Nevada* (reprinted by University of Nebraska Press, 1985). As an insight into a hard rock miner's travails, there is a Scots Gaelic saying that, drawn to a quest for buried riches, miners "*dannsa leis an diabhal.*" They dance with the Devil.

Still standing, the ghost town of Bannock's rustic church.

A New Century &
a New Year

In the mountains, rangelands, and deserts of the Far West, the turn of the twentieth century was an occasion for uncertainty and apprehension. What lay in store? Was mining on the skids, with reserves of gold and silver nearing exhaustion? And what about cattle, an industry founded to feed miners? The only sure thing appeared to be the fate of Indians, settled down and resigned, if not happy, on their reservations.

And so it was, that not only was the turn of 1900 of concern, but that of 1901, 1902, 1903 and now, 1904.

In cities, towns, and camps large and small.

And this takes one to Bannack, long ago and briefly Montana's capitol, population at the time a hundred or so, where in the mid afternoon of December 31st, a wagon was backed up to the entrance of the Methodist church, so that a dozen townspeople might cart the house of God's pipe organ – not a melodeon, but an honest-to-God pipe organ – out the door, and transport it over hill and dale to a barn at Swanson's ranch.

The organ objected, as did Miss Delilah Dahlquist, the church's organist. Rocks and bumps in the road prompted sour notes and wheezes, cause for shouts from little kids and cries from stray fowl. Before the instrument could be unloaded, Miss Dahlquist was up in the wagon and working its bellows.

As she feared, the response was awful: a half a dozen shriek-ing, stuck notes.

But then she was reassured and to a degree calmed by learn-ing that a mining pump man from the up-country camp of Red Mountain would be attending their New Year's night dance. If he couldn't tame the dissonant contraption, no one could.

Indeed, at that very moment a batch of Frasers were on their way by buckboard from little-account Red Mountain. They paused to freshen up. Father Donald whisked dust from his go-to-meeting (and only) suit. Daughter Mary primped; her two brothers passed a cracked mirror one to the other. What Billy might have seen could well be the likes of a portrait he would in time ink on the gourd of his homemade violin.

He appears nattily dressed, in a jacket over a high-collared shirt. His jaw is clenched; he has a swept-back, abundant head of hair. As his crusty father might have decried, "More the poet

than the miner, that's what he's become."

Come dusk, they'd made it to Swanson's barn, to be greeted by a cheer from the better part of Bannack's population, and the relief of Delilah Dahlquist, who, once her instrument was repaired, sounded the chorus of a familiar hymn.

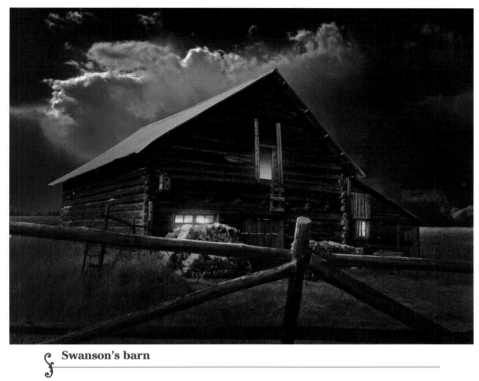

Swanson's barn

Assembled for a candlelit dance. A somber hymn was not what they
had in mind.

As they milled about, Billy Fraser, now in his twenty-forth year, took the measure of the crowd – different folk than back in Virginia City. They didn't dress fancy; they were happy in homespun and calico. Certainly some fine young ladies here. But there was something about the men, their eyes. Was it a guarded wariness, suspicion? It's as if, without warning, they could suddenly turn on you. Which, Billy realized, was only to be expected considering where they were.

Hard by Montana's outlaw country.

Hoofbeats! The barn's crowd hushed as the other half of the night's orchestra appeared in a cloud of dust, reined up, and dismounted. The crowd cheered, and cheered all the more as Kid Trailer unsnapped a pasteboard case, and brandished his violin.

Considering that posters offering an $800 reward were plastered throughout Silver Bow County, the Kid was remarkably cavalier. And everyone knew (or had convinced themselves) that he wasn't all that bad. His outlaw moniker reflected his role as a herdsman for the notorious Ieuch-Jones gang (indeed bad), hailing from Montana's wooly Big Muddy Canadian borderlands.

Miss Dahlquist was wary of this fellow musician, only to have her apprehension abate as they discussed what songs to play, what keys to use, and how the jauntiness of his fiddle could provide a counterpoint to the hum and heft of organ pipes. An unlikely duo to be sure, but there was no other choice.

They played and, to everyone's delight, played well! The Kid carried the tune, and like a dance partner, Delilah followed his lead. When they knew the words, folks in the crowd would sing along as they played ballads of Nelly Bly and Jenny Lind, or the popular "Star of the Evening."

Young Billy, overcoming a Scotsman's innate reticence, would have ventured dances with Bannack girls. And mopping his brow in intervals between awkward scottishes, mazurkas, and waltzes – of which he had only vague notions – he would have struck up small talk of whether a snowstorm was in the offing, of grizzlies raiding larders, of the prospect of new strikes off in his camp of Red Mountain – while all the while furiously wondering what life would be like if fatally charmed by the opposite sex.

He imagined life with an Ella, Effie, or a Mabel.

He was presentable, was he not?

But then, the barn door flew open, and there he stood. Sheriff Nick Moore, back in Bannack after escorting a miscreant to the new state prison up in Deer Lodge.

The boy working the organ's bellows froze. A chord wavered and died away.

"Jack Winnefield also known as Charles Winfield, known as well as Kid Trailer, you are under arrest for numerous offenses of which you and all Montana are well aware."

A Scotch Ballad.

The miscreant, however, had the wits about him to accompany the Sheriff's charge on the violin, and cap it with a glissando and jaunty trill.

"Kid, do I have your promise that you'll behave?"

"Yes Nick, I do."

"Then you may ride your own horse, and retain possession of your instrument."

The Sheriff was backed up by a deputy bearing a flaring pine pitch torch. They marched the Kid from the barn.

And, somewhat stunned, the evening's company of New Year's revelers watched as the torch bobbed this way and that, and vanished in the woods at the base of the barn's hill. Billy Fraser didn't know what to think, but then it came to him: Kid Trailer was all right, indeed he was a fine fellow. Gallant, polite, talented.

An ideal, a figure to be admired? Not really, but an interesting thought.

"Happy New Year, I guess" someone half-heartedly uttered. Indeed, midnight was nigh and the gathered crowd listless, and feeling, well, cheated.

"Sheriff Moore has no right to do this, no right."

"Maybe yes, maybe no." And with these words, a plot was hatched. By now, the Sheriff, his deputy, and the Kid had a fifteen or twenty minute lead – that could by overtaken by a shortcut known to rancher's daughter Sally Swanson, a spunky lass with an ace cutting horse. In no time, a dozen riders were plunging down the road to the town, but then veering off on a barely discernable track. Hooves trampling underbrush, they raced through a forest, galloping rather than walking their horses, as the law and its quarry was sure to do.

The shortcut intersected the main road connecting Bannack with the outside world. The party wheeled about, horses panting, and waited. And sure enough, the torch born by the Deputy was headed their way.

"Not unexpected," said Sheriff Moore as he neared the riders blocking the road. His horse pawed the dirt. He hesitated, then continued, "And who's to say you shan't have your dance?" He smiled. Kid Trailer flashed a great grin. The Deputy wasn't sure what to make of this, but gamely went along with the Sheriff's command to lead the way back.

Up by the barn, a little girl, up way past her bedtime, spied the torch, and shot inside to inform the townsfolk. "Johnny, man the bellows," Delilah Dahlquist ordered. And he did, getting up a head of wind, to be expended in a mighty diapason fanfare.

And presently, Kid Trailer, joining in, was fiddling and sawing away.

Throughout the early hours of 1904, Sheriff Moore checked his pocket watch, first by candlelight, and finally by dawn's early glow. His deputy was a mass of yawns. And the Sheriff noted that Delilah Dahlquist was tuckering out, which prompted him to walk over, incline his head in a bow, and offer his hand. Delilah was not a spinster, not just yet. She closed the organ's keyboard. The Sheriff gave Kid Trailer a shout, "Carry on!" Which the Kid did, now toting a chair to the center of the barn's floor, and bowing his violin as one might a cello, that he might call out the moves of a country reel.

"Sashay your partner! Do-see-do!"

They did, dancing round and round. The Sheriff and Delilah, everyone. They stamped and whooped, circling the Kid as sunlight now streamed in the barn's open door. Whirling by, they cast him in shadow, then light, then again, shadow.

A number of Bannack's adventurous children had climbed the barn's rafters, and looking down, had a grand view of the kaleidoscopic, spinning spectacle below.

As the sun climbed the sky of the first day of 1904, the family Fraser – dad, two sons and a daughter – were on their way to their home and mine in Red Mountain, Montana. But they didn't get far, as in the driver's seat Alexander, after stifling several yawns, fell sound asleep. A brief consultation, and they headed back to Bannack's surprisingly elegant Hotel Meade, there to rouse a clerk with clangs on a front desk bell.

"Yes? You'll be wanting…?"

"We come from the dance, and find ourselves in need of a few winks."

"Then up our grand staircase you go, and pick any rooms you like. You'll be the only ones here."

"And the tariff?" inquired Donald.

"For just a nap, you say? No charge."

"Why thank you," offered sister Mary, "and friend, may you have a Happy New Year!"

"May we all, may we all," the clerk nodded, shuffling off, rhetorically mumbling, "though I haven't the slightest idea what that might entail."

Bannack's Hotel Meade, still standing.

BEADLE'S
Dime
New York Library

COPYRIGHTED IN 1888, BY BEADLE & ADAMS.

ENTERED AT THE POST OFFICE AT NEW YORK, N. Y., AT SECOND CLASS MAIL RATES.

Vol. XXXIX.   Published Every Wednesday.   Beadle & Adams, Publishers, 98 WILLIAM STREET, N. Y., May 16, 1888.   Ten Cents a Copy. $5.00 a Year.   No. 499

IT WAS SULPHUR SAM. WHOOPING AND YELLING HE DASHED AWAY UP THE VALLEY AT BREAKNECK SPEED, FIRING HIS REVOLVERS AS HE WENT.

OR,

Sulphur Sam's Double.

A Romance of the Wild Lands of the Yampah.

BY J. C. COWDRICK,

AUTHOR OF "RAINBOW ROB," "KENTUCKY JEAN," "BLUE-GRASS BURT," "GILBERT OF GOTHAM," "THE GIANT CUPID," "BROADWAY BILLY" STORIES, ETC., ETC., ETC.

CHAPTER I.

"HANDS UP!"

FAINT but clear rung out the silvery tones of a cornet, waking the echoes of the mountain wilderness with one of Foster's most plaintive airs, the notes reverberating from hill to hill and dying away at last in the valleys and canyon.

It was in Northwestern Colorado, in the wild region north of the Yampah River and near the Little Snake River whose united waters go to form the majestic Colorado.

The time was twilight—that mystic hour

Imaginary desperados inspired real-life outlaws.

On the Banks of
the Big Muddy

For Billy Fraser, it had been a night and dance he'd long remember, one that would chart his course for years to come.

There'd be no further lament of: "Just wrap me up, and throw me away." He'd make something of himself. He'd cut a figure that folks would remember – and dammit, respect. Two things impressed him.

One. Kid Trailer was a Kid. And what did that mean? Coming down on the wrong side of the law? And so what if it did?

Two. The Kid's violin. Billy loved the sound: jaunty, plaintive, sweet, hopeful. It prompted a tumble of emotions. Could he learn notes and the wonderful chords the Kid had bowed? Maybe, maybe not. Reading and writing had been hard enough.

Over dinner back in Red Mountain, Billy announced his intention to heretofore be considered a Kid, prompting his father to blurt, "We don't need a Kid in the family. It was enough that you entered the world in the year he left it."

"And who might that 'he' be?" Billy ventured.

"Billy the Kid, off in Lincoln County, New Mexico," his father replied, "Granted he was a charmer, a nice dancer, even what you might call a ladies' man. But you see, he was malignant and cruel, possessed as he was by a spirit as hideous as hell. He reveled in brutal murder and gloried in his shame. You admire the likes of that?"

His son stuttered, "No-no, of course I don't." But Kid Trailer was different, was he not? So it was that after a decent interval and considerable thought, Billy announced he would like to try his hand at prospecting the country north of Red Mountain. As the Fraser's mine tunneled directly into a hill, the operation didn't require a shaft, and could be worked by two men. And whatever Billy found and staked, he promised, his father and brother and Mary too would receive a share, the equal of his.

Truth was he knew at the time he had little care for prospecting gold or silver. Rather, he was drawn to Big Muddy Creek up by the Canadian border – and its raffish Kids, its outlaw renown.

Not that there weren't Kids nearer at hand, on the road north. In the copper camp of Anaconda, there was – or rather had been – Kid Flanagan, shot in a squabble a few weeks back. And further on, there was the Pancake Kid, a cook for desperado George Bird, but otherwise innocent enough.

♪ **The late Pigeon-toed Kid.**

In searching out Kids, Billy hit upon a handy trick. He'd randomly inquire as to the "whereabouts of the Kid." And folks would respond accordingly, naming this-or-that fellow.

Which, though too late, led to the Pigeon-toed Kid, J.C. Brown, a horse thief gunned down by the local sheriff. For his last words, he'd asked for a pencil and paper, but lost consciousness and died within the hour.

Groomed by an undertaker and on display down by the train station, Pigeon-toed looked positively beatific – and gave Fraser pause in his quest.

Nevertheless, he tramped on, beyond the end of the rails, beyond the reach of the law. On up to Big Muddy Creek, a headwater of the Missouri River, and refuge for, among others, Butch Cassidy and the Sundance Kid. The Wild Bunch.

He thought of seeking them out, finding his way to their Hole-in-the-Wall hideout and making their acquaintance, but didn't quite have the nerve. Instead, he veered north and west, to a spread owned by one Harvey Logan, Kid Curry.

He approached the spread's ranch house, and finding the door ajar, stepped inside.

"Hello..." he ventured, and was answered, "Hello yourself" by a dapper little fellow who materialized in a doorway across the room, a man recognizable in a well-known photograph of the Wild Bunch. But he no longer ran with the Wild Bunch; he had gone off on his own, and could boast that fully fifteen of subsequent killings attributed to the Wild Bunch had instead been at his hand, the hand of Harvey Logan, Kid Curry.

What had Billy gotten himself into? Should he flee?

Snake-eyed Kid Curry took his measure – and unexpectedly, offered Billy a drink.

In a photograph taken a few years earlier, the Sundance Kid is
seated lower left, and Kid Curry stands upper right.

Billy nodded, and noted over the Kid's shoulder, hung on
pegs, a violin and a banjo.

For lack of anything else, he asked, "Do you play?"

"I do not! I in fact hate music, whatever its form."

"I see," Billy nervously responded, though he didn't see at all.

"Them instruments belong to my kid brother Lonny. But understand, he's not a Kid – capital K – *like me*. You want to see
what that entails?"

With no idea what he was in for, Billy nevertheless nodded.
Upon which the capital K Kid fished a poker chip from his
vest pocket, placed it on the back of his hand, and raised it to

shoulder level. "I'm going to drop it, and you're going to count how many shots I get off before it hits the floor. Understand?"

Billy nodded. Best not to say anything, just nod.

With that, Kid Curry drew a revolver from inside his jacket, and flipped the chip.

"One-two-three!" Billy exclaimed, as three shots spun the poker chip this way and that.

"Remarkable!"

"It's nothing," the Kid allowed, compared how I can make a fellow dance. "Want to see?"

"Can I take your word for it?"

"I suppose. Now about that drink, bourbon all right?"

Anything would have been all right. And Billy was to note that the Kid's mood could shift in an instance, from bellicose to mellow, and back again.

Somewhat later that day, a two-horse shay delivered Annie Rogers (or Della Moore or Maude Williams, whatever name she was going under) to the ranch house. As a prostitute working in Madame Fannie Porter's brothel in San Antonio, Texas, she had caught Kid Curry's eye, at the time on the lam after robbing a Colorado & Southern train. The pair had become romantically attached, and here she was, up for, well, a visit.

"Out!" the Kid ordered his brother Lonny, present at the time, "and you too," meaning Billy.

They obliged and, biding their time, strolled the bank of Big Muddy Creek. Their talk turned to Lonny's violin.

Queried Billy, "Is it hard to learn it?"

"Depends on your feel for it. Truth be, I don't read music. But I do understand scales and keys. And I have my instructors…"

♪ **Annie Rogers and Kid Curry**

At which Lonny cocked his ear, and listened as an oriole sang, perched on a branch on the far side of the creek. "Captivating, you might say, even dazzling. You see, at least to me, what livens a tune is its embellishments, the likes of trills and glissandos. Listen!" It was now a goldfinch's turn, and the tiny bird gave the larger oriole a run for its money. Next, there was a pizzicato thrush, then a dove, cause for Lonny to exclaim, "Hear that! Damned bird is playing chords!"

So began a first lesson, with more to follow, as with Annie-Delia-Maude and Kid Curry off drinking – or who knows, holding something or somebody up – Lonnie dared fiddle on the ranch's front porch, and coach Billy as he tentatively followed suit.

At Billy's prompting, Lonny recounted the outlaw life of the brothers Curry, the Kid, Lonny, and Johnny, before Johnny got himself killed. It was a life fueled in by heavy drinking, the Kid's violent temper, and his nose stuck in "yellow backed literature," the nickel and dime novels of the day.

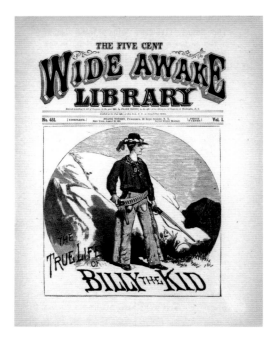 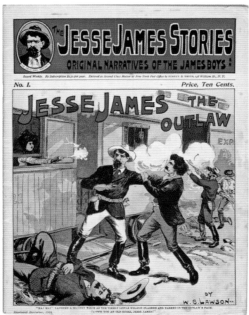

There were outlaw heroes to be imitated, even surpassed, out-gunned. The truth was that the brothers were doing well enough in the cattle business, but when it came down to it, they were more interested in being bad men.

"You too, you as well?"

"'Fraid so. Let's face it, it's fun to 'hurrah' a saloon, riding in on our horses and shooting up the ceiling, even when a horse went through the floor and wound up in the cellar. And once, busting in on a dance, Kid Curry didn't like the music, prompting him to bash a guitar over a fellow's head." Lonny paused, then added, "That explains why when the Kid's around, my violin and banjo hang yonder on their pegs, gathering dust."

Billy nodded. He understood.

"Would you want my violin?" Lonny asked of a sudden, "Fiddlin' and shootin' being kinda, what's the word… antithetical."

"No, no, good Lord no," Billy replied, "but thank you very much anyway."

Though of course he wanted the violin, at the time down from its peg and resting on a chair on the far side of the room.

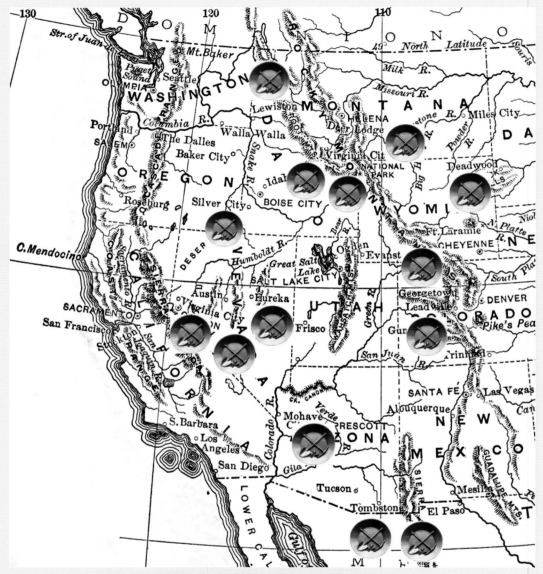

The desert West in the early 1900s – and major stops on its "tramp circuit."

Tramping
the Camps

Come June of 1904, five months after the Bannack New Year's dance, Kid Curry was dead, cornered by a posse after a Denver & Rio Grande train robbery, wounded, then choosing to shoot himself in the head rather than face capture. As for his brother Lonny, Billy Fraser may have been in touch with him – or not, there's no knowing.

It's also unclear whether the link between Montana outlaws and sudden death gave Billy second thoughts. Probably not, considered that his preferred appellation from now on, his father be damned, would be "The Montana Kid."[4]

In any case, for his return to Red Mountain, Billy, now a Kid, had rehearsed an elaborate explanation of his misbegotten prospecting, only to find this of little interest to his father and brother. In his absence, Donald and Alex had worked well together, quite well, until their ore pinched out, and was exhausted. That was a problem with mining. Gold and silver were

---

[4] The obvious appellation would have been "Billy the Kid," but that already taken, our Billy was likely inspired by an earlier "Montana Kid," rustler and dynamiter Isaac Granville, known for precipitously riding off on "anything that has hair."

finite, and once gone, were gone for good. But now they'd come up with a plan.

The Frasers, Dad, Alex, and the newly-minted Kid, would become "tramp miners."

Tramp miners? Sounds low grade, dregs at the bottom of the mining barrel. And there were those who reviled them, calling them "RALs, Ragged-Ass-Leasers." What they'd do is show up in a town or camp, and offer to work a specific underground area – typically 100 by 100 feet – of this or that level of a mine. For a set amount of time, it would be all theirs. And they'd not be paid, but rather split – fifty-fifty – the proceeds of what they found with the mine's owner, who otherwise had nothing to do with them, other than grumble and fume as to what ingrates they were if they pulled up stakes after an initial, slim-pickings ten day commitment.

"Avoid these gypsies as you would avoid fire," a newspaper of the day advised.

"Drunks, thieves, low-life" they were – until they next showed up, and a renewed deal was negotiated.

"Think of it," Donald could well have mused, "Good ore and we rake it in. Bad and we're on down the road. The country we'll see!"

But Mary, what about sister Mary? It appears she had her share of living rough, and had set her sights on the new Nevada camp of Goldfield, where there was an abundance, it was said, of well-paying positions for women.

As for Donald, Alex, and Billy, they'd heed the call of the next big thing, wherever it lay in the peaks and valleys of the Far West.

Deadwood

A town named for a stand of dead trees clumped in a gulch – that was presently the site of a scattering of bawdy houses. The lure here, however, was not so much the *doves du prarie*, but rather the gold of George Hearst's Homestake Mine. Its main shaft was now over five hundred feet deep, with no sign of its rich ore giving out.[5]

Though the Homestake's miners had no particular love for Mr. Hearst, they were adamant as to anyone threatening their jobs.

For the Frasers, the next move would have been to shrug the place off, and tramp south into Colorado.

Leadfield & Georgetown

Here were rival towns, both proclaiming they were their state's "Queen of Silver." If one didn't work out, the other would.

Hopefully.

In Leadfield, a sign in a saloon asked: "Please do not shoot the pianist. He is doing his best." Regrettably, it applied as well to the city and its mines, all but played out.

---

[5] The Homestake in time would plunge 8,000 feet into the earth and become the deepest and richest gold mine in North America.

On to Georgetown then, that from a distance appeared substantial and prosperous, with imposing brick banks, mercantiles, and schools. But on closer inspection, dirt-streaked, broken windows signaled abandonment. And where were the crowds, reported to have thronged the city's streets – and toasted their good fortune at the Hotel de Paris?

A look inside was to confirm a depressing reality: the boom was over.

There appeared to be few, if any paying guest.

Creaking footfalls stirred clouds of dust.

Corridors and rooms echoed faded elegance.

Someone was about though, off in the kitchen. He was a baker brought to Georgetown by the hotel's founder, M. Louis Dupuy. Though the hotel no longer served meals, he had appreciative customers for his fresh brioches, croissants, and French breads. Too bad about the silver running out, but that's no reason why people shouldn't eat well.

If a conversation was struck up, he might well have compared his calling to that of the Frasers. "You blast rock; I knead dough. And the more rock you blast, the more silver you have – until, *quelle surprise, c'est fini*. But my goods, they are forever, beloved by *prince ou paysan*. And gold and silver, are they not but *servantes de vanité?*"

The Frasers would have gotten the drift of what he was saying, and could well have seen the truth of his dour assessment. Nevertheless, they needed to eat, and may have considered that even in a failing camp, there is a last option for a miner – to, as with the Union Mine back in Virginia City, "put out a mine's eyes," extracting pillars rich in silver that had shored up tons of country rock. With luck, you'd make it out before an inevitable collapse.

Risky, yes – but then again, excellent pay.

"You're in need of men to rob pillars?" Donald would have queried a mine manager.

And if so, as a team, the three Frasers would have dropped down a shaft to a hollowed-out stope.[6]

With great caution, even holding their breath, they would have blasted one pillar, then another, then another, with every flare of a match a step closer to oblivion. "Makes you wonder," the Kid was to whisper, "What's the point of all this?"

"All of what?" Alex whispered back.

"Now that I think of it, all of it, all of hard rock, precious metal mining," blurted the Kid, "silver for fancy ladies' candlesticks and teapots, gold for chains and watches tucked in the vests of Eastern swells. You know, Astors, Vanderbilts and the like, fond as they are of bathroom gold faucets, gold flushers, gold …"

"Enough," rasped Donald as he lit a fuse, then hastened away, his sons following.

---

[6] A cavern once chockfull of high grade ore.

It was a relief to dodge the Devil and make it to the surface. "You're right, son," allowed Donald, "We do indeed do what we do for avaricious bastards. So where would you next like to go? Maybe it will be different."

"Eureka, there's Eureka," volunteered the Kid. Off to the west and plumb in the middle of nowhere.

Eureka

After a long and wearisome journey across Utah and well into Nevada, the Frasers would have been heartened by their first glimpse of what had been described as the "Pittsburgh of the West." What to others would have been grim and depressing – barren heaps of slag and a belching smokestack – signaled a smelter refining ore. And where there's still ore, there's still a good chance of caging a lease.

Better yet, the Frasers would soon learn that there was a problem in water flooding the nearby Ruby Hill mine. A massive Cornish pump had been shipped from a defunct mine in Virginia City, and there were problems getting it up and running.

Who better to save the day than the (self-described) renowned pump man Donald Fraser, and his stalwart assistants, the Kid and Alexander?

They settled on a place to stay, and may well have remained in Eureka for at least a year or so. They didn't mind its godforsaken air and location, and their work wasn't all that hazardous. Indeed, they were advised, the major hazard in town was the cat house of Madam Henrietta Lake, a self-styled "Terror #1" for central Nevada, on one occasion threatening to "carve up and wipe out an entire neighborhood."

On up the social scale, Eureka boasted an opera house (not that an opera was ever performed), a fine place to enjoy, on holidays or no holidays at all, frequent dances and balls, often lasting the night through.

Oddly, Eureka was a family town, with a share of young women, virtuous and not. And tarrying here – while other tramp miners came and went – offered a perspective on what desert camps were worthwhile – and which, as the Frasers tramped on, to skip. With rotten rock and little regard for safety, Delamar, Nevada, was downright dangerous, earning its nickname

A masquerade and a local belle (or she might have been a visiting entertainer).

"The Widowmaker"; a fellow who'd been there wisecracked that funerals were so common that gents daily donned black coats and women wore black frocks. And appropriately, Tombstone, Arizona, was as dead as a bone yard, thanks the recent flooding of the Tough Nut Mine, with nobody sure what to do about that. Likely, its ore had slipped from good to marginal.

Bisbee, Arizona, a day beyond Tombstone, was thriving, though for the Frasers mining the camp's copper, what pennies were made of, would be a notch down.

Bisbee

What the Frasers hadn't counted on was that Bisbee had become a hotbed of IWW – International Workers of the World – unionization, with threats to, among other things, bring on their Mother Jones, the nemesis of hard-hearted mine owners.

No surprise, Bisbee's miners – *Wobblies* – were a sullen lot, with little interest in welcoming the likes of the Frasers.

Even so, Bisbee was to figure in what, for decades to come, would be a tramp miner's anthem:

> The miners come from Bisbee,
> The timbermen come from Butte,
> The muckers come from
>   Coeur d'Alene,
> So throw some lagging down
> my chute.[7]

> Up this road I've been before,
> No one will ever know.
> And I missed the path,
> And I can't go back,
> And no one will ever know.

---

[7] To explain: *Timbermen* built elaborate "square set" structures to prevent, or at least forestall the collapse of a mine's drifts (tunnels) and stopes, in the process laying waste entire forests. *Muckers* shoveled freshly-blasted ore into handcars. And *Coeur d'Alene* is a silver mining region north of Wallace, Idaho.

There's a sadness to this – a lament of men trying to find their way, but fated to missing the path – and who knows of this, or who cares?

A related, wishful (rather than morose) sentiment is inscribed on the foot of what would become the Kid's homemade violin:

> To Me as I Travel the Desert Track…
> A Blushing Maid From a jolly Troup – Is all I Lack.

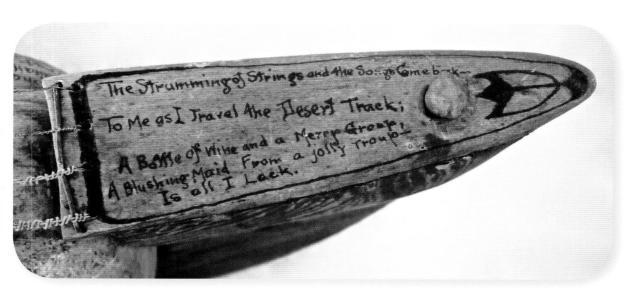

But wait. The Frasers would next heed the siren call of Oatman, Arizona, a camp that had boomed before, and was on the verge of booming again.

With prospects – who knows? – of a Blushing Maid.

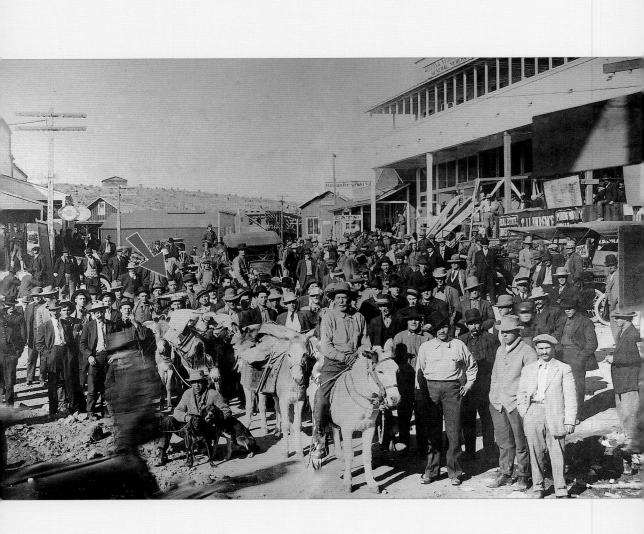

La Violetta

Arizona east of the Colorado River was written off as "a mean ash-dump landscape." That is, until a single word changed everything: *Gold!*

The Frasers would have been drawn here, driven in good measure by desperation. Their success in working the tramp circuit had been, at best, marginal. There had to still be good ore – pay dirt – somewhere. And the burgeoning camp of Oatman could be that somewhere.

First thing in the morning, lensman N.E. Johnson had set up his camera, and given a high sign to Lou Grossman, better known as (with affection) "Lou the Jew." He's in the photograph (arrow) and holds aloft a megaphone with which he'd rounded up quite a crowd. Prospectors and their burros. Miners. Uncomfortable in suits and ties, money men looking for a slice of the action. Stock promoters intent on "hanging paper" (peddling worthless claims). Lawyers, self-proclaimed experts in mining matters. Plus the likes of butchers, bakers, and candle-stick makers (with the camp's mines demanding thousands of candles a day).

The Tom Reed Mine, a lodestar for footloose miners.

What's here is a population on the move. Miners were not the only ones tramping a circuit. So were they all, all these men, and women too, one way or another, lured by glittering, beckoning gold.

Oddly, there don't appear to be any women in the crowd. Some may have been *otherwise occupied*; others may have had concerns about *respectability* and *appearances* (rare words in a mining camp).

The photograph taken, the crowd would have broken up. Organizer Lou would have headed back to oversee lunch at the Oasis Café, one of his enterprises.

The Frasers would have been off in search of work for experienced tramp miners. Circling Oatman, a hundred shafts were being sunk, some real, some imaginary, chimeras of shady stock promoters.

A block or two from the center of town they were implored by a woman, a striking woman, "You men, you're all together, yes?"

They nodded.

She indeed was quite a lady, from her dancing shoes to her wild coif of black hair. She was garbed in riot of red chiffon ruffles and colorful cloth flowers, with beneath this (the Frasers would see, but not just yet) knee-length purple and black striped trousers.

"I am *La Violetta the Wire Dancer*. Perhaps you've heard of me, perhaps not. In any case, until yesterday I had a helper, a coot who pitched in to put up my rig, and with his concertina gather a crowd and accompany my aerial act."

"Might you boys lend a hand?"

The Kid, Alex, and Donald looked one to the other, shrugged and smiled, and were forthwith stringing a thin metal cable from a second story window to one on the other side of the street. "No need to fret about the concertina," she said over her shoulder as she flew upstairs and struck a pose in the window, "I've a plan."

Meanwhile, quite a crowd had gathered, and gazed upward as she set foot on the wire (and the need for her knee-length trousers was evident).

La Violetta, wire dancer extrodinaire.

"My friends down there, as gold-seekers all, let a song of you calling be the music of my performance." With that, she sang – and danced.

> "Unclouded skies bend o'er us;
> 　　Yon mountains, rich in hidden gold
> 　Lie temptingly before us."

She steps onto the wire, and without a pole, balances on single foot.

> "We need no Midas' magic wand,
> 　Nor wizards rod divining;"

She runs, really fast, over the street.

> "The pickaxe, spade, and brawny hand
> 　Are sorcerers in mining!"

She spins about, and bows.

"Want to see more?" The crowd roars. And the show – and the song – goes on. She leaps high in the air; she reclines on the wire; she does a handstand; she does a head-over-heel flip. Finally, a fluffy red blur, she does a dazzling three flips in a row.

She exults, "I feel my happiness up here! I'm so happy! As you all, in time, will certainly be as your labors enrich you!"

With that, she swung down from her wire, and from a traveling trunk produced and passed a flower-decked hat (curiously, several sizes too large for her head). The Frasers then helped dismantle her rig, and were off to see just what Oatman's prospects might offer, the Kid excepted. Asked if she might join him for lunch, La Violetta had accepted his offer.

There was a line stretching out the door of Lou's Oasis Café, waiting for a table, but neither minded, for they were to dine in "the Delmonico's of Oatman," as Lou was fond of stating.

Finally seated at a table and unmindful of its greasy oilcloth, slopped soup, and scattered crumbs, they chatted. The Kid was curious as to La Violetta's past, and came up empty hand-ed. The best he could elicit was her real name: "Edith." As to his past, he recalled his words as a kid (small "k") in Virginia City, "Just wrap me up, and throw me away," but chose not to share this. Today, in the company of a beautiful woman, he felt very much the better of himself.

In common, their eyes and dreams looked to the future. On his part, the Kid was considering parting with his father and brother, and going it alone as a "D.P.," a desert prospector. La Violetta might be happy high in the sky, but he was anything but happy underground, with hundreds of feet of country rock over his head. Prospecting, he'd get to roam where he pleased, and if he found anything, he'd dig no more than a few feet, file a claim, then unload it on a willing buyer. God knows there were enough of them: "flash company of the dandy class." They'd crowded the picture taken that morning.

La Violetta flopped a postcard on the table, not of her, but of a famed wire dancer, Princess Victoria, renowned as "the Lady in Red." It seemed she was the star attraction of the Sells-Floto circus, scheduled to arrive by train and play Las Vegas ten days hence. La Violetta would see what she was all about, and possibly angle to succeed her, as she was but the latest in of a series of Sells-Floto ladies in red.

"What do you think? Am I her equal?"

"Better, I'd bet."

At this juncture, proprietor Lou appeared tableside, to offer the pair a dessert on the house. "Cherry cobbler." And he gave

them his card, with under his name the line: "Wind Blew, the Bull Flew, See Lou."

"And just what does that mean?" La Violetta asked.

"I've no idea," replied Lou, "But it's catchy, don'tcha think?"

Over dessert – quite tasty – the Kid proposed a plan. "You have a week before you're on your way, and need some help putting on your act. And I for one could stand some company wandering the desert. What say we link up? In the morning or whenever, you dance your wire. And after that, we prospect the nearby desert."

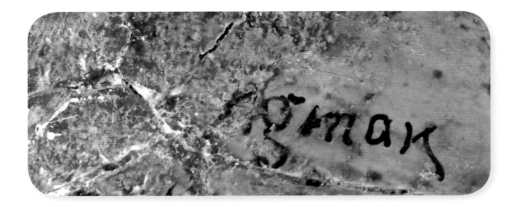

"I'd like that, yes I believe I would."

And so the next day they were on their way, playing nearby Goldroad, Milltown, Mohave City, and Hardyville. And in one instance, panning good color and then spending an afternoon erecting piled stone corner markers and a center monument to a claim, its name, and theirs tucked in a tobacco can.

The claim was for the "Edith V." And a day or so later, it was filed in the Mohave County seat of Kingman, its courthouse attested in a partially legible word on the Kid's violin.

Was there a touch of romance to this fleeting partnership? There's no knowing. Yet consider verses close by "Kingman" on the gourd.

Curved around the gourd, the words are difficult to read. They ask:

> How Shall We know that the Songs are Sweet?
> How Shall we know They are Friends we Meet?
> First, That the Heart of the Singer is Pure
> The Other: Ah! The Touch of the Hand of the Sure,
> They Will We Greet.

Were the Sweet Songs La Violetta's? Did the Kid believe her to be pure of heart?

Was he delighted by her sure touch of the hand?

The Kid was to sadly see La Violetta off, bound for Las Vegas on a three-times-a-week stage. And as well, he bid father Donald and brother Alex goodbye, as they now headed north to reunite with sister Mary, who, they were heartened to learn, had done quite well as an assistant to a Goldfield stockbroker – and had a lined up a choice of mining leases of interest to Donald and Alex.

Might the Kid's and Violetta's paths again cross?

He hoped so.

She was, in the argot of the day, "the real Tabasco."

A celebratory shipment of Death's Valley gold.

Death's Valley

Now on his own, the Kid was off to Death's Valley (as it was once called), and by whatever means he could – be it in the back of a buckboard or by ankle express – he was on his way to Rhyolite, an outpost of civilization prior to a plunge into Death's Valley. If anywhere, many believed, great stores of gold, silver, and copper lay hidden there, awaiting a prospector's pick. Was it not logical – that nature would have stashed great treasure in this, the hottest, most fearsome place on earth?

Regrettably, there wasn't the slightest logic to this.

Nevertheless, the Kid was heartened when from around a bluff on the road to Rhyolite he heard music. A violin – and a harp! A wagon hove into view, bearing a two-man orchestra and bedecked with a banner proclaiming that a first shipment of gold ore from the Bullfrog mine was on its way to a San Francisco smelter.

The Kid waved; a man with a rifle perched behind the musicians waved back, as did the driver and armed guard of the treasure wagon that followed.

In Rhyolite, the Kid stocked up on supplies and negotiated the purchase of a burro. The creature was female. What to call her? Sadie? Lizzie? He settled on "Violetta," that he might every day be reminded of his wire dancer.

Over Daylight Pass, and then down, down, and more down, the pair went to finally set foot on the Valley's salt caked floor, to then cross to the Panamint Mountains on its far side. Fortunately, the Kid was not alone. He'd fallen in with another prospector; together they trekked a landscape "eighty feet from hell."

Crossing the Panamint Mountains was a challenge. Fortunately, the Kid had a map, helpfully marked with the best places to prospect. It led him to a rocky pass, then down, down to

another valley, parallel to Death's, to finally sight the camp of Ballarat, named after a famed strike in Australia with the hope that its success would rub off on whoever fetched up here.

It was reputed to be a "place of little order and less law."

King Street, Ballarat

Walking the camp's King Street, the Kid took note of his and the burro Violetta's shadows – and another, that would presently overtake them. It was cast by an unusually large fellow. He was talking to himself, apparently in the throes of composing a poem.

> It is men of brain who go insane,
>   And men of soul whose souls are sad.
> And men of heart?... They're driven mad.

Clarence Eddy, "togged up," possibly to tout a mining claim.

"*Mad!*" he exclaimed to himself, "That's the ticket! Rhymes nicely with sad."

He'd drawn abreast of the Kid. "O, hello. My name is Clarence Eddy, famed, at least in some circles, as 'the Poet-Prospector.' In recent years incarcerated in the Utah Asylum for the Insane. Thirsty? Care for a drink?"

Forestalling a reply, he pointed the way to the Headquarters Saloon, down the street and to the right.

They paused as the Montana Kid tied Violetta to a hitching rail, and the Poet-Prospector rattled off another verse –

I do not know there is a hell below.
    I know there is heaven above.
The hell that is here is the one I fear.
    I hope the hereafter is love.

"I'll certainly drink to that," volunteered the Montana Kid.

And that said, they entered a dingy, decrepit saloon, its one touch of elegance, a pool table at the far side of the room.

"You're looking at the only one between Rhyolite and the railroad town of Mojave," proclaimed the man behind the bar. The Kid blinked.

Despite the heat, the fellow wore a swallow-tail coat, starched celluloid collar, bow tie, and a bowler hat. "The name's Chris Wicht. What'll it be, gents? Warm beer or tanglefoot? Tanglefoot's a whiskey."

What was this place, this town? Clarence picked up on his puzzlement. "Newspaper up in Goldfield ran an article on us, said that hereabouts was "the world's largest underground insane asylum.' But I take issue with that. Should have made that '*above* or underground. Both!' You agree, Chris?"

"I do. Indeed I do."

Somewhere outside, someone began playing a violin. Barkeep Chris Wicht rolled his eyes; Clarence versified, "Is it not the siren voice of sin, with her tilting violin?"

The only known photograph taken inside the Headquarters Saloon. It must have been an off day for Chris Wicht, as he's dispensed with his customary formal attire.

Ballarat's mystery violinist.

"Dunno who that fellow is, nobody does," said Wicht, "Showed up a week or so ago, and fiddles away as if life here is an old-time gaslit melodrama."

The Kid peered out the window. Maybe the violinist, whoever he was, was right about that, as with the coming of the night, Headquarters regulars stopped by and were introduced by Clarence, oft called the "Big Man." There was the "Short Man," prospector Shorty Harris, in the company of his friend Jim Sherlock, a man with a penetrating steely-eyed look, that of a gunfighter about to draw. Shorty allowed he once was one, adding that when there was a surfeit of chickens in town, they'd line them up, and "Jim, at twenty paces, would shoot off their little heads. Never miss."

"Right, Jim?"

No answer, unless you count a clench of teeth and a curl of the lip.

Clarence endeavored to lighten things up with, "I think we should care for one and another, and our animal friends too ..."

He was cut short by the blare of a front seat Victrola, and then the rasp of a needle skittering across an Edison disc as outside Doc Woillard hit the brakes of his motorized long-bed,

walk-in *Monark of the Desert Princess Radium Health Car No. 2*.[8]
He sauntered into the saloon. "Anyone sick, in need of irriga-
tion or radiation? No? Good! A double for me!

"Your usual…"

"My usual," confirmed the desert quack.

With dusk at hand, Chris Wicht made the rounds of his Headquarters Saloon, lighting kerosene lanterns, and ushering in an
eve the Montana Kid would fondly remember.

No surprise, there was prospecting talk, of one's ability to
"feel" or "smell" rich ore. Of the pursuit of "float, blossom, and
structure."[9]

There was a question of a prospector's "luck versus pluck,"
with the assertion that luck can be good – and bad. Take the
case of Concantentious Bill. His was cussification bad.

Good and bad luck – did they run in streaks, like quartz or
porphyry?

Were there lucky charms? Like a favorite pick, a shiny nug-
get – and in one case a Bible, which prompted the telling of
the tale of H.H. White, who on a Sunday read the Holy Book
in the shade of scrub pines atop a fifty-foot cliff. Drowsing,
he dropped the book, and with a start, witnessed it tumbling
over the precipice. Down in a canyon, White discovered it lying
face up, opened to Matthew, chapter 7, with a sizeable piece of
quartz, dislodged by the fall, having torn a jagged hole in the
seventh verse familiar to all Christians, especially if they were
prospectors.

---

[8] As to the Victrola, it was the equivalent of an ice cream vendor's tinkling
bells. It alerted prospective, ailing patients.

[9] "Float" is rock dispersed down a hill from a "blossom," a surface showing of
promising ore. "Structure" is the geological look of an area.

Ask and it shall be given you; seek and you shall find;
knock and it shall be opened to you.

Believing this a good omen, H.H. White searched and in just a few minutes located the rock's parent ledge. It was two feet wide, and assayed at $225 per ton.

"Hallelujah!" Doc Woillard exclaimed, seconded by shouts from regulars like Shorty and Jim, plus nightfall arrivals the likes of Hot Steam, Deef Bob, and Bessie, a formidable lady prospector.

Shorty Harris (center) welcomes visitors up from Los Angeles for an ersatz taste of the Old West. That's his home, Ballarat's abandoned schoolhouse.

Near midnight, they dispersed, but not before someone commented, "A church. One of these days we should consider a church."

Alas, in all its years, Ballarat never got around to raising a church.

Actually prospecting?

When they had to, they did. To pay for food and drink, to get by. "But you should be here New Year's eve," Clarence told the Kid, "and a midnight deadline for making a hundred dollars worth of improvements on a claim in the previous year. There's all manner of scurrying around and setting out for destinations unknown – with the intent of jumping this or that claim."

Otherwise, it was drink, then prospect and camp, and in the rare instance you found anything, peddle it to whoever was handy, and be off to Goldfield to blow what you made – and be back in Ballarat, pockets turned out, penniless. As garrulous Shorty would bend a visitor's ear, "Who the hell needs $10,000,000. It's the game man, the game."

But then, at a point where the Kid hadn't gotten to first base in that game, word was out that newly found gold – possibly Breyfogle's legendary gold – had been struck on up in the Panamint Range, overlooking Ballarat! Assays were off the scale, though nobody was exactly sure who had run them. Overnight, prospectors from near and far swarmed Ballarat, with their legion including a number of Kids from as far distant as Goldfield, home of the Dogface Kid, Kid Foley, and Kid Highey. Closer by there was C.M. Wadell, the Greenwater Kid and Ed Bahten, the Furnace Creek Kid.

Huffed up, the Montana Kid had no use for them, the lot of them, with the possible exception of one or two of the Goldfielders. What had they done to distinguish themselves? Shoot up saloons? Rob banks and trains? Rather, they were crummy cutups – *cut-ups*, that was the word – prone to mischief, not mayhem. They were different, way different, than Kids of the Big Muddy up in Montana – in the fear they engendered, in the respect they got.

Ironically, the only Kid new to the camp that merited the name was to be found in a comic strip in a newspaper left behind in the Headquarters Saloon. He was the Yellow Kid, and though fictional, was everything that a Kid should be. His yellow nightshirt boasted, "He wont call me no tender feet no more."[10]

At this point it might be noted that, until now, the Montana Kid himself hadn't *really* done anything that bad or outrageous.

That was to change.

In its glory days, such as they were, Ballarat had boasted seven saloons, but now was down to two, Chris Wicht's and across the way an establishment run by one John Chambers. The Montana Kid had knocked down a few drinks there, but had found the place dreary and depressing.

[10] "The Yellow Kid" was America's very first comic strip.

Chambers was all bluster, self-importance, and ignorance. And the Kid didn't care for the way he mouthed "Kid," whether it be with a dismissive shrug or a sneer verging on a snarl. That got to him. Time to take him down a notch.

The Montana Kid sharpened his pocket knife and screwed up his courage. He ruminated on what he might say later that afternoon. And to his surprise, the answer was "Nothing." Action would suffice.

Striding into Chambers' Saloon, he set a foot on the bar rail and called out, "Your best whiskey. Make it a double."

"Kid, like it or not, we only offer a single whiskey. Comes in barrels."

He filled a glass, plunked it down. The Kid grasped it, held it up to the light, and then – quite unexpectedly – upended it, puddling the bar and splattering Chambers.

Sputtering a confabulation of curses, Chambers reached for a rag to mop things up and then eject the Kid, only to put him in range of the Kid's left hand grasping his beard and with his right hand flipping open his pocket knife and hacking it off!

The Montana Kid snapped the knife closed, dug a dime from his pocket, and slapped it on the bar. He turned to leave, and unfurling his left hand, trickled a trail of gray hairs across a spit-stained floor and out into Ballarat's blazing, cracked-earth sunlight.[11]

Uttering not a single word.

---

[11] The Fraser-Chambers confrontation is affirmed in George Pipkin, *Ballarat 1897–1917* (Lancaster, California: Paul B Hubbard, n.d.), p.72.

As news of this got around, the Kid noted a newfound respect when not only his Ballarat friends, but outright strangers addressed him. A reverence, even.

As for Chambers, he would no longer be "John" or even "You there." To his dying day, he'd be called "Whiskers."

Otherwise, it didn't take long for Ballarat's boom – a desert humbug, one of many – to lose steam and expire. Life returned to normal – normal for a population of loonies.

As for the Kid now, running low on cash, there was a need for some serious prospecting, no more puttering in the Panamints. And accordingly, he was periodically away for weeks, even months at a time.

Always there was anticipation and suspense as he ran field assays. If, when heated, samples produced frosty white beads, he'd roll them in dampened salt and expose them to direct sunlight. If blackened streaks appeared, there was a chance (but no certainty) he'd struck silver.

If a sample was dark and heavy, he would heat it to redness, ever hopeful that a vaporous white cloud would rise – an indication of black gold.

The Kid staked claims from Cold Spring in the Saline District down to the Coso District, where he filed on a promising "Copper Chief Lode."[12]

And every time the Kid returned to Ballarat, there were fewer and fewer old timers haunting the Headquarters Saloon.

---

[12] In the years 1907-08 members of the Kid's family may have visited him in Ballarat and prospected as well. His older brother Alexander, teaming up with poet-prospector Clarence Eddy, sought the riches of the "Nitre Lands" in southern Death Valley.

He would ask them, "Anybody with any thoughts as to where a fellow might go? Next?"

There were few suggestions. The one that stuck was: "There's the El Paso Mountains, well south of here. Some years ago there was a city there – 'Ophir'– same as where in the Bible, King Solomon got his gold."

"So I've heard," a fellow agreed. "And nobody's been there since."

With which bartender Chris Wicht was to murmur under his breath, "For good reason."

Ballarat stalwarts: "Single blanket, jackass prospector" Shorty Harris and one-time gunslinger Jim Sherlock.

Bad news for a lone prospector.

Lost Ophir

Trekking south from Ballarat, the Kid and his burro had a vast, sere landscape pretty much to themselves, stretching as far as the eye could see. Violetta was happy; there was ample and apparently tasty forage. The Kid was wary. Not about the Paiutes rumored to roam the land; he rather liked Indians. But about water. Springs were scarce, dried up, or not to be trusted.

It was a relief, then, to sight the El Paso Mountains, and in their foothills make it to Mesquite Springs, a jumping off point for what once was Ophir City. Indeed, there was a stove-in adobe nearby, apparently a supply depot for workings higher up in the range. The Kid investigated, and was surprised to find shelves of canned goods, intact kegs of Giant Powder, and tin files of mining records.

Hoofbeats, approaching. He stepped outside, saw a buckboard, slowing now, driven by an elderly, affable gent. "Jacob Kurhts," he said, alighting, "and I wouldn't have thought to find another soul here."

"Me neither," said the Kid.

It seems that this Kurhts had once been a stage driver, his route the road up from Los Angeles, and then on to mining ventures in the Slate Range, over toward Death's Valley. "I was young, I'd say younger than you."

And way back then, returning to Los Angeles with an empty stage, he'd been attacked by Indians. "Injured one of my mules. But I outran them, only to spy a few skulking about in a wash just out of sight from where we presently stand. And, just like today, it wasn't just me here. There were two other men, down from Ophir City. One was mine superintendent George Yarbrough; the other was C.W. Tappan, a stock promoter and newspaper correspondent. I suggested that they *not* spend the night here, but rather over at Desert Springs, better fortified in the event of an attack."

"Sound advice..."

"But Yarbrough, he poo-pooed the threat, and stayed on – as Tappan and I moved on. And here's where the story gets inter-

♪ **The locale of Superintendent Yarbrough's murder.**

esting. The next morning Tappan was on his way out of the desert. And I returned here – *with Yarbrough nowhere to be found.*"

The Kid cottoned to the story, reminiscent of a dime novel.

"Now, you might ask why I am here. Getting on in years, I'm writing up a memoir, and want to see if there's anything I've overlooked or missed. In any case, back then I spent the whole day looking for Yarbrough. No luck. And no luck the better part of the next day, when anxious as to the fate of their boss, Ophir miners arrived and by torchlight continued the search through the night and into the following day."

"And?"

"It didn't end well."

Half a mile away, they found him at four that afternoon. George Yarbrough lay dead, horribly mutilated, his remains piled with stones. On examination, a bullet had been fired from

a large bore rifle, striking his stomach. A smaller bullet had caught him in the shoulder, and his right arm had been shot through from his wrist to his elbow. A revolver had been emptied into his right side and his right leg, shattering it.

"His body was so battered and broken that his miner brother could do no more than roll it in a blanket, sling it on a burro, and carry it away up the mountain, to bury it on a slope up from Badger Springs."[13]

"And you know what?" Kurhts continued, The Yarbrough Company back in L.A. came to the conclusion that this was not, as first might be expected, the work of Indians, but the work of white men, at least two of them considering the different bullets destroying the man's life and body. And who might those white men be?"

Before the Kid could think of anything to say, Kurhts answered: "Those white men had to be myself and C.W. Tappan. And over the years, the accusation has plagued me, despite an L.A. judge dismissing the case. And that's why I'm here." Saying that, he fetched a sheaf of papers – evidence he had accumulated – from his buckboard.

There were a surprising number of newspaper articles, given this was a crime off in a lonely land. Yellow clippings chronicled…

> Mines are furnishing very flattering prospects with owners confident of a rich harvest. The abundant springs promise the nucleus of a great city, poco tempo.

---

[13] Superintendent Yarbrough's brother worked in Ophir City's mines.

> The El Paso district was coming out rapidly. Large sale
> of stocks have just been made in L.A., and the owners,
> instead of gassing to get stocks up are working to get
> the gold out, which strikes us as sensible.

> We have all had the "ups and downs" of prospectors –
> have been here in the sunshine and the storms, have
> passed through all the vicissitudes of searching for
> Eldorado. Sometimes we have felt amazingly rich, other
> times have thought to surrender the ship. But now
> gold ore has assayed for as much as $4,340 a ton; silver
> lodes up to $4,220 a ton.[14]

"Those second and third notices were written by C.W. Tappen. Poor fellow, heard he got shot in the face in Deadwood back in '78. I'd hoped he might bolster my case, my innocence."

A last clipping…

> There is not a single soul in the district. Fact is, the
> place was discovered by poor men, with no influence,
> who were driven away by the Indian war.[15]

" 'The Indian war,' doesn't that tell you something? That they were on the warpath, commencing right here?"

The Kid nodded, agreed.

In any case, Jacob Kurhts was here to see if there was anything that might shed further light on the killing – and at last, clear his name.

And indeed, there was.

---

[14] The clippings are from the *Daily Alta Californian*, 1863, and the *Visalia Delta*, 1863 & 1864.

[15] *Daily Alta Californian*, 1866.

The map was likely compiled with the intent of promoting stock sales. On it, two routes are marked from Mesquite Springs to the Ophir Mining District (upper right), one a wagon road and the other a short-cut burro trail.

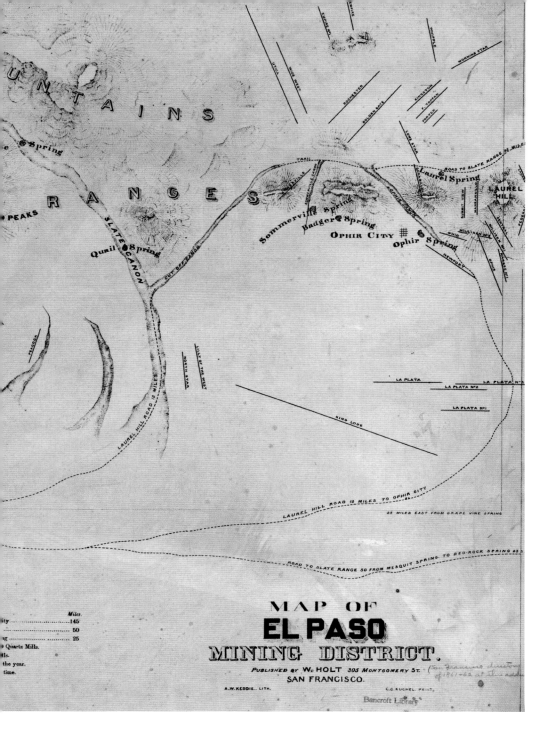

MAP OF
EL PASO
MINING DISTRICT.

PUBLISHED BY W. HOLT 305 MONTGOMERY ST.
SAN FRANCISCO.

A.W.KEDDIE. LITH.　　　　C.C. KUCHEL. PRINT.

In the abandoned adobe by the spring, there was a tin box that had been shipped to promoter-prospector Tappen. And in it was a map, actually some twenty maps, all identical. They were sizeable. Rather than roll one out on the adobe's dirt floor, Kurhts and the Kid examined it in the back of the buckboard. The Kid marveled.

It was a treasure map, a compendium of gold, silver, and copper in the El Pasos.[16]

Kurhts was heartened. "Think of it! If I or Tappen or both of us had done poor Yarbrough in, why was the entire range – and dozens of mines marked of the map – abandoned within a year? No! This was clearly the depredations of Indians, armed not with bows and arrows but with contraband firearms …" He trailed off, adding "I made my case, but who listened, who cared?"

The Kid shook his head over the injustice of it all – but chances are, he was distracted by the thought of all those mines, all those claims. All now lapsed, all ripe to be jumped. And there was the matter of the last known Ophir assays: in a single ton, $4,340 in gold, $4,220 in silver.

The Kid and Kurhts parted, with the Kid and Violetta now following an abandoned track up into the El Pasos. It didn't help that the higher they got, the stronger the wind.

Dark clouds crested the Sierra Nevada Range to the west. It began to rain, and not gently.

---

[16] Of interest: the Kid's sister Mary had staked a claim on Black Mountain, the principal peak in the map's uppermost "Range of Burnt Mountains." Had her experience contributed to his interest in nearby Ophir City?

Violetta stumbled on the rain-slicked slate, time and time again. The Kid cursed the trail clogged by sagebrush, and higher up, blocked by rockslides.

As it does in the desert every few years or so, the sky opened up, as if someone up there was emptying a giant bucket. And finally, after close to three miserable hours, they came in sight of a mine's derelict gallows frame, then another, then more on the flank of Laurel Hill to the east. There were crumbled buildings as well, the remains of Ophir City.

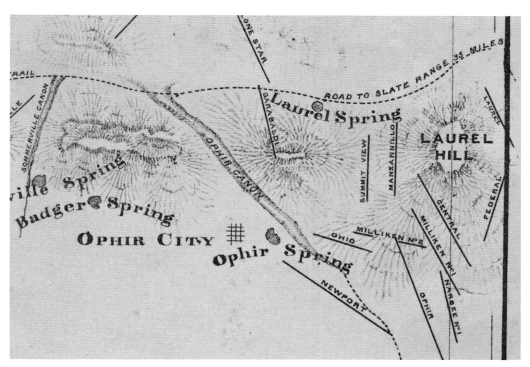

Detail of the El Paso map – and a dozen nearby mines. George Yarbrough was buried an unmarked grave located at the "O" of Ophir City.

In a similar mine's abandoned shop.

Only a single building offered shelter, its rippled tin roof more-or-less intact. Though a door banging and squeaking in the wind, the Kid stepped inside. The roof leaked; the floor sloshed. He was in what appeared to be a workshop for nearby mines.

Outside, in the rain and howling wind Violetta brayed. Not one to be heartless, the Kid led her in and tethered her to a rusting drill press.

And it came to the Kid: this was the place, or at least it would do! For months now, he'd thought he might create… a violin. Indeed, while in Ballarat, he'd mail-ordered a Sears horsehair child's bow (32¢) and a packet of violin strings (12¢). Further, over by Saratoga Springs in Death's Valley he had picked out a choice coyote melon, ideal (well, better than nothing) as a violin's sounding box.

At Cold Spring up in Saline Valley, he'd even whittled a cottonwood peg, then another three.

Before him now was a last requirement, wood. Racks of it in all shapes and sizes. And not just pine, but flawless, first-rate redwood.

With night falling, the Kid found a lantern and amazingly, an intact can of kerosene. He cleared a workbench and rustled necessary saws, planes, files, and even useable sandpaper.

Throughout that night, with rain drumming the adobe's tin roof and Violetta the burro looking on, his violin took shape.

Come dawn, or what would have been dawn if the sun was shining, he was about done. He looked about for a can of varnish, only to find its contents stiff and solid. No matter, a finishing touch could come later, or not at all.

Tentatively, he drew the bow across the strings. The cry of a strangled cat! But wait, he'd neglected to soften the bow with Paris rosin (Sears, 3¢).

Another pass with the bow, and that was more like it. On the squeaky side, but what could he expect? With an alacrity that surprised him, Fraser essayed a verse of "The Miner's Song," a gold-seeker's classic. His performance was capped by a peal of thunder and the echoing calls of two ravens circling a landscape of wreckage, decay, abandonment.

And here and now, he decided it was it was time to move on from the Kid stuff. He'd be more, far more than a cutup, harebrained Kid. Scarier, ruthless even. He grasped his violin, and on the flank of its coyote melon gourd, inscribed:

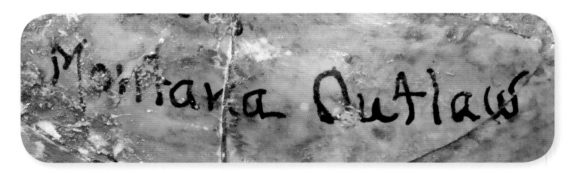

It was pouring, harder than ever, as the newly assumed Montana Outlaw strode outside, and his violin tucked under his jacket, ascended the hill beyond the adobe to what the

꧁ **Dead mesquite mark the site of Badger Springs.**

map had labeled "Badger Springs," appropriate he thought, "Badger" being a nickname for Cornish miners (he being half Cornish).

And twenty yards uphill from there, he came upon George Yarbrough's hastily dug grave, piled with rocks to ward off marauding coyotes.

Leaning into the wind, counterpointed by ravens' calls, he improvised a lament. It was sad, sad as sad could be. The Montana Outlaw had first meant his tribute to be cheerful, but it didn't come out that way.

𝄞 **Yarbrough's last rest.**

Trekking back down to the adobe, he now had second thoughts about his assertion, a hour ago, that he would henceforth be "The Montana Outlaw."

Just what had he been thinking?

When it came down to it, there was no escaping the truth: Be they white outlaws – or in this case, depraved Indians – desperados were a blood splattered, despicable lot.

Back inside Ophir's crumbling adobe, he gave Violetta a pat, wiped his violin dry, and bid the place farewell. Slipping and sliding in the incessant rain, man and burro descended the El Paso Mountains. His intent had been to angle east to the sleepy little town of Shoshone, California, there to find a buyer for the burro Violetta, and with the proceeds, catch a train on up to Goldfield, and the welcome company of Alex, his father Donald, and his sister Mary.

But that was not to be.

Dusk, the Mojave Desert.

Oh Rip, Rap,
Flick Flap

That afternoon the drenching rain moved on and the sun made a welcome appearance, prompting Billy to change his plans. He'd veer north to tarry a day or two in Ballarat, there to drink up and commiserate with his prospector friends, hapless though they might be. Indeed, Chris Wicht's Headquarters Saloon would have a cozy appeal in the wake of the gloom and despair he'd encountered in the El Paso Mountains.

The sun set, and the desert was alive with the calls of creatures who had laid low during the rain.

As he sought forage for Violetta and scrub for a campfire, Billy enjoyed the hoot of an owl, the howls of a passing pack of coyotes, and brays in response from Violetta – and felt, why yes, he too was a creature of the desert, with his newly crafted violin his call, his song.

A "song dog" coyote – as on Billy's violin.

He fleetingly considered adding to his "Montana Outlaw" inscription. Beneath it, there was room for two or three lines of doggerel, perhaps something on the order of "a fast-on-the-draw legend of the West." But hell, he didn't even have a gun. Rotating the violin he painstakingly inscribed a dedication to what in truth he was.

A "Lonely Desert Prospector."

The violin is signed "Very Truly W.H. Fraser" with the addition a modest title: D.P., presumably "Desert Prospector." His inscription is down-to earth and humble, and poses the question: who are the "Others" that he as a prospector makes happy? Eastern investers and speculators? Not if he could help it. A lost love, Violetta the wire dancer? Perhaps. It would be nice if their relationship had survived their time back in Oatman. She would have wowed the crowd in Ballarat! He thought of her as he unrolled his blanket under an inky sky and gazed at the sight of stars, stars he could almost touch.

Then, just as he was nodding off, Billy saw a twitch on the far side of his campfire – of a shadow cast by a tiny kangaroo rat on its nightly rounds.

Away across the desert, a lone coyote howled, cause for the rat to leap and sail through the air, over the fire, over Billy and his blanket. And then scurry off. *Jeezle-beezle, shot from a cannon!*

Might there be a lesson in this? Might it affirm that the desert – not what was buried beneath it – was a truly wondrous place, creatures included?

In any case, in coming days, Billy Fraser would care not a whit about Ophir's unmined ore, its fabulous assays be damned. He recalled Shorty Harris's oft repeated: "Who the hell needs $10,000,000. It's the game man, the game." And even so, what was so great about "the game"? *What indeed was so great about gold*, other than the grief visited on men (and women too) engaged in its lustful pursuit?

Enough of gloom. Enough of chasing geology's "blossom, float, and structure."

On his way north across the desert – to many a prospector, a desert of dreams – Billy didn't heft or examine a single rock.

On his revisit to Ballarat, Billy boarded Violetta at Tom Biggin's corral, and headed for the Headquarters Saloon, on the way passing Whiskers Chambers, who, to avoid him, skittered to the other side of King Street. Billy reminded himself that here he'd been feared, and had fleetingly gained the respect due a fellow on the wrong side of the law.

In his absence, things at the slap-dash saloon had changed; the pool table had been moved away from the wall. In its Ballarat tenure it had been a place for bets over who would sink what ball, the site of a night's snooze, and now a stage – with the poet-prospector Clarence Eddy its current attraction.

There wasn't all that much to Ballarat. Tom Biggen's corral is off to the left.

**Nattily turned out,
the Poet-Prospector.**

No surprise, he was over at the bar chatting with Shorty Harris. He welcomed Billy, and was intrigued by his coyote melon violin.

"You made that thing?"

"I did."

"And you can play it?"

"Clarence, I can indeed. In fact, camped out over the last few nights, I've garnered the accolade of coyotes."

"Then I offer you not one, but two drinks if you accompany me this eve." With which he leapt up onto the pool table, which audibly groaned with the impact. He was, after all, the camp's "Big Man." He gestured for Billy and his violin to roost by a corner pocket.

With Billy's strumming of strings, the crowd at the bar hushed and in the course of the next hour, gave ear to Clarence's declamation and Billy's fiddle.

Clarence cleared his throat, and whispered to Billy, "The tune is Kipling's 'Absent Minded Beggar.'" He hummed a snatch of the tune, Billy nodded, and the Big Man boomed, with an equally big voice –

I'm goin' to Thunder Mountain, where the golden
    nuggets grow,
Where the miner's big percishun gets in swing.
I'm goin' to Thunder Mountain, where the balmy
    breezes blow,
And the snows of winter vanish in the Spring.[17]

How the camp will be a hummin', and all hands
    imbibin' booze,
How the blasts will be a boomin' on the air,
How the mules will be brayin' as they hear the
    joyful news
That the boys are findin' nuggets everywhere.

This was the desert's promise, Billy well knew, even as he
was now forsaking the idea. At the end of additional verses,
Clarence's poem concluded:

I'm going to make a fortune without fail!

But then, Clarence shook his head, as if in sorrow, and saying
nothing, turned away from the crowd. His shoulders slumped.

Billy sensed the Big Man's change of mood, and bowed a
run of dissonant chords.

Clarence swiveled back to the crowd, his visage ashen –

I have been to Thunder Mountain, and I'm busted flat
    by jing,
On mining matters I have changed my mind,
I did my very darndest, but I didn't strike a thing.

---

[17] Thunder Mountains are found in several western states. The one
Clarence had in mind was likely in Idaho, where he was born and over
the years had prospected.

And worse yet –

> Five thousand I then invested, in Golden Chariot stock,
> When all at once she took a flop. They couldn't find
>   pay rock!

"And there's a chorus to that," he continued, and invited the crowd to harken to –

> Oh rip, rap, flip flap.
> I wish I had my money back
> I'll deal no more with mining stocks.
> I'll be a wiser man.

The chorus was less sprightly, and more a dirge with each succeeding hard luck verse. "My God," Billy well might have murmured, "This be us, this be me."

Again, the refrain, with a raggedy crowd joining in –

> Oh rip, rap, flip flap.
> I wish I had my money back
> I'll deal no more with mining stocks.
> I'll be a wiser man.

There were further dour, downbeat poems, one lamenting –

> All things are given to him that hath gold –
> All of the comforts the world doth contain –
> All are controlled, bartered and sold,
> Heaped up by avarice, hoarded for gain.

This concluded –

> Heaven alone is the hope of us all,
> Hoping for Heaven we meekly endure,
> For up in Heaven, so we are told,
> *All is not given to him that hath gold.*

The boys at the bar and surrounding the pool table nodded their heads, muttering the likes of "If there is a heaven…" and "The way of the world, I suppose." Others studied their alkali-encrusted, scuffed boots, and had nothing to say.

But Clarence was not to leave the pool table on a downbeat note. In a welcome change of pace, he recited a lively –

> Black eyes beaming
> Brown eyes gleaming,
> Gray eyes sweet and true.
> All are fair,
> Though none compare
> With Abbie's eyes of blue.

Billy knew not of Abbie – or if she even existed – other than her offer of –

> Sweetest kisses,
> Rarest blisses.
> Mortals ever knew.
> Oh to hold you,
> And enfold you.
> Abbie, I love you.

Heartened to an extent, the crowd offered huzzahs, though muted huzzahs considering that the night's entertainment had lamented their calling and life's work. In any case, Clarence theatrically bowed, then turned to acknowledge Billy, who bowed as well.

Alighting from the pool table, Clarence propelled him to the bar, there to whet their whistles with warm beer and tanglefoot whiskey.

Stepping out into the moonlit night, the two parted company, but not before Billy thanked the Big Man for including him in his performance, and sharing his insights.

"Here in broken-down Ballarat," he mused to himself, as he walked away on down King Street, " I've confirmed what I've come to feel about gold, life, and what have you – from the lips of a man recently released – or maybe even escaped – from an insane asylum. A madman." Billy looked heavenward to the moon and stars.

> Oh rip, rack, flip flap
> Have I been a wayward chap?

Try as he might, he couldn't come up with what to say or rhyme next.

And this would be the last he'd ever see of Clarence.

Billy would be up before dawn, and on his way across Death's Valley to burgeoning Rhyolite, there to regretfully part company with his burro Violetta, and hop a Las Vegas & Tonopah train north to Goldfield.

A few years hence, the poet-prospector Clarence Eddy would again be committed to the Provo, Utah's asylum for the insane, there to spend the final fifteen years of his life.

His last communication was a scrawled note –

You Must
Remember
That I Am
Absolutely
Lost
Beyond
All Possible
Recovery.

C.

Goldfield, Nevada, proclaimed "the Greatest Gold Camp in the World."

The Mohawk Saloon & the Way of the World

Illuminated by ropes of Edison bulbs, Goldfield's Main Street glittered in the night. A few blocks away in the adjoining settlement of Columbia, Donald Fraser and his son Alexander had taken over and fixed up a forsaken bungalow. And within walking distance, sister Mary was ensconced in a modest Goldfield bungalow.

The family united for a celebratory dinner at the tony Palm Grill, though celebratory of what no one was sure.

The Palm Grill was on down the street. The Mohawk Saloon was off to the left.

Billy then opted for a cigar and a solo stroll to the "cross-roads of the West," an intersection boasting four renowned saloons: The Northern, the Palace, the Mohawk, and the Hermitage. He ambled into the Mohawk.

A four-piece band with a big-hatted lady piano player was taking a break. There was a faro layout to the left, and a craps table to the right. Most everybody present was looking – glaring – his way. Tobacco spit splattered the floor. The place stank.

An odd little mousy fellow nudged Billy's elbow. "I give

Roundly ignored.

them names," he said, "The Faro dealer, he's a tough nut, a 'Buster.' And the sweaty craps man, I'd say he's a 'Waldo.'"

"Allow me to introduce myself, I'm S.W. Erdnase." The man was soft spoken and talked through his nose, in Billy's experience, a sign of a con, a confidence man.[18] "Regard the Faro dealer," this Erdnase continued, "Note anything out of the ordinary?"

"Not really, excepting the blocks under his chair legs."

"Perceptive!" Erdnase hissed, snake-like. "Then note how these blocks allow him to rest his arm flat on the table – and manipulate a 'hold-out.'"

"A hold-out?"

"Yes. It's an up-the-sleeve rig that allows him to switch out a card, a pair of cards, or even an entire deck, though this last requires great skill, enviable skill. You might note how the dealer regards us. A defiant look, yet with a hint of fear."

---

[18] An S.W. Erdnase, was the author of *The Expert at the Card Table*, an early 1900s manual of how to cheat at cards. The name appears to be a pseudonym, possibly adopted by a card shark of the day, E.S. Andrews. (Note that S.W. Erdnase spelled backwards is E.S. Andrews.)

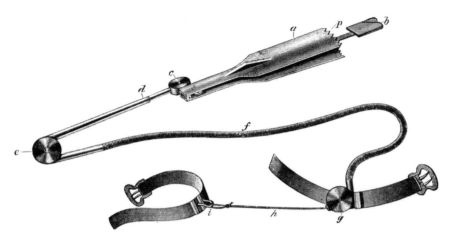

[Here is what a hold-out looks like, a diagram lifted from a San Francisco "Advantage Goods" catalogue peddling marked cards, loaded dice, and crooked gambling devices.]

Erdnase next suggested that Billy direct his attention to the Mohawk's craps table, and its dealer. "Waldo over there, he as well looks in our direction, fear also in his eyes. And justifiably so, for look behind him, and you'll see the man leaning back in his chair and intently gazing in the dealer's direction, with his right hand likely holding something in his lap. And that, I'd wager, would be a mariner's compass that with the dealer in need of a six, would spin 180° as the dealer hit a concealed switch that activated electromagnets tucked beneath the table's felt. And the dice being loaded, they'd land with sixes up, a pair of them."

*[Here's how the dealer's
dice could be loaded.]*

Billy was dumbfounded as Erdnase whispered, "As to the apprehension in the man's eyes, suppose the man behind the craps dealer – or an irate Faro mark across the way – now jumped to his feet and dragged a dealer outside, even shot him. For good reason, dealers get twice the pay of miners, for they as well could be dealt death's hand."

"There's no honest gambling?" Billy seriously wondered. Erdnase gestured that they step outside.

A crowd had gathered, and for what? To have their picture taken by Goldfield photographer Arthur Allen.

After that, the men lingered. To place bets. *On anything.* Who could hock a goober the farthest. Would the next woman to round the corner be a blond or a brunette? Where was that rat scurrying?

"All honest," Erdnase assured. "Even so, some are lucky, extraordinarily lucky." He drew Billy's attention to a singularly odd fellow.

"Call him 'the Pumpkin,' in that he resembles one. Notice how, time after time, his wagers pay off. He's a rare exception to the way of the world.

"The way of the world," Erdnase repeated. "And that is that all fortune is random, unless, as we've seen tonight, the deck is manipulated, or the dice loaded. Rigged, artfully rigged."

This S.W. Erdnase was getting on Billy's nerves. What did he stand for? Whose side was he on? Dealers or players, *call them sharps or call them flats?* He turned to pursue this… only to discover that Erdnase had slipped away.

Vanished in the desert night.

Walking the mile to his father and Alex's Columbia home, Billy shook his head over the chicanery of it all. In a way, it was like prospecting; you'd anticipate striking it rich, the same as you might place a bet on the turn of the card. And cash in? Rarely, if at all.

As he stepped through the door, Alex inquired, "How'd you do, Kid?"

"Very well, actually. Didn't win anything; didn't lose anything; learned a lot."

Donald looked up from reading the *Goldfield News*, and an article quoting a prospector running down the camp as a sink of "gold, greed, and corruption."[19] And you know," he agreed out loud, "it kind of is." With his pipe, he gestured to the bungalow's fireplace. Billy's violin was on the mantle.

"Over there. Is that your doing?"

"It is."

"Good work, excepting it's inscribed 'Montana Outlaw.' Last I heard, weren't you the 'Montana Kid'?"

"I was, but tell you what: there's no need to call me either one. From now on, I'll be sticking with 'Billy,' or even 'William,' if you like."

Donald relit his pipe, and reflected on the quote in the newspaper. "Let me ask you two, can you imagine *greed* and *gold* in the same sentence?

With "Certainly can!" and "O yes, for sure," Billy and Alex agreed.

"But then, how about *greed*... and then let's say, the word *violin*? Billy?"

---

[19] Despite a population nudging 25,000, Goldfield was never considered a city, but always a camp. And the prospector in question would likely be "Death Valley Scotty," a mean, windbag fraud. The best that could be said of him was that he was "the fastest con in the West."

Note the addition of a bicycle bell – to give Billy's strummings a cheery zing-bing-clang.

"In the same sentence? No, not that I can see – or, really, even imagine."

At which, father Donald hummed... the introduction of the familiar "Song of the Tramp Miners," a cue for Billy to fetch his homemade violin, and provide accompaniment, all now singing –

> Up this road I've been before,
> No one will ever know.
> And I missed the path,
> And can't go back,
> And no one will ever know.

And there was a surprise to this. Sung with a remarkable gusto, the baleful lyrics were transformed. They were cheerful, jubilant even, accented with the tremolo and clang of the bicycle bell Billy had purchased in a mercantile across from the train depot.

Donald rose from his chair, to proclaim, "*Je suis prest!*"

Brothers Billy and Alex were puzzled, other than realizing the words were French.[20]

"It's an old clan motto," Donald explained, "the rallying cry of the Frasers. '*I am ready!*'"

---

[20] The Frasers were said to migrated to Scotland from Anjou, France. Their name may have been derived from the word *frasière*, "strawberry."

"I am ready,' Billy agreed, though not sure for what. Not to prospect for gold and silver – but okay, he supposed, to free it from the earth, and earn a decent four dollars a day, a miner's going rate. He'd had enough of a hit-or-miss lifestyle.

He'd join his family as they heeded the desert's call.

Across cracked alkali plains.

To faraway hills, and beyond.

Inbound to Eureka, Nevada.

The Eureka Opera House

The steam engine "Eureka" was as close as a machine can come to having a personality, chuffing and huffing through Palisade Canyon to its namesake town. There was a time it hauled a dozen or more carloads of treasure seekers; now a single car made a daily run, and often was near empty. Aboard today were four Frasers.

Father Donald, brothers Alex and Billy, and their sister Mary – after some deliberation, they'd agreed on Eureka as to where they'd like to settle down. Or give it an honest try.

It made sense. Gone were the days of "The gilded palaces of vice. The nefarious gambler, the dreaded gunslinger, are memories only; their day is past, their race is run."[21] But there was now an appeal. Gone were the clouds of foul smoke and ash spewed by fourteen smelters. The air was clear, the town was picturesque, even charming. And there was plenty of ore yet to be mined, decades worth, for it was now lead that was at stake, not fickle deposits of gold and silver. Gone as well was the greed that lights the eyes of stock sharks and speculators.

---

[21] C.W. Torrance, *History of Masonry in Nevada* (Grand Lodge F.& A.M., 1944), chapter XIII.

The majority of the population appears to be in the parade, not watching it. Note the ten-piece brass band; did music's muse have a foothold in Eureka?

A final benefit: though many camps claimed to be "in the middle of nowhere," none were as remote as Eureka – and as welcoming to experienced miners, or for that matter, anyone at all.

By happy coincidence, the Frasers arrived on the eve of the Fourth of July.

It was a festive day, and for the Frasers a productive one. They got wind of a house up for sale, furniture and all, by a family calling it quits and moving back East. And strolling the town's boardwalk, they saw there was truth to the boast (or decry, take your pick) that "every other building is a thirst parlor," with Cramer's Saloon currently the subject of choice gossip.

Therein, it appears that Hogeyed Mary had knifed a belligerent fallen angel, Bulldog Kate, who as she expired allowed, "Hogeyed Mary, the bitch has killed me, and I think I deserved it."

Best of all, slaking his thirst at another saloon, Billy Fraser struck up a conversation with a fellow who, as luck would have it, was a shift superintendent at a nearby Ruby Hill Mine.

"You're a pretty good miner, are you?"

"My dad and brother as well."

"You all check with me in the morning. We'll see."

Eureka miners – the likes of the Frasers.

Five miners coordinate in lighting a twenty foot span of fuses that will blast loose thousands and thousands of dollars worth of lead ore.

With a storm threatening Eureka, good reason to stay inside.

Over the next few weeks, the Frasers could hardly believe their good luck. They were game for work, hard work, and that they got. As a fellow in the cage hurtling down to the 2,000 foot level asserted, "It ain't nothing easy."

But then spirits were raised – and miners offered bonuses – as 2,450 feet on down they holed into a massive deposit of ore that was an astounding 30-40% lead.

"Well I'll be damned, a goddam bonanza! Just when you'd least expect it."

"Best since way back, in the 1800s!"

At the end of a shift, the Frasers would relax in their spacious parlor. Everybody had their chair, their favorite chair.

Billy would play his violin. They'd sing, struggling to keep up with the little instrument's wobbly grasp of keys.

"We do the best we can with what we got, is that not so?" offered Alex. "As in music, as in life."

Come Christmas morning that first year in Eureka, Billy descended the stair, helped himself to a cup of coffee brewed by Mary and shuffled to his designated chair, to discover it occupied by a violin, a *Gasparo Da Salo*. Sear's best![22]

---

[22]An unusual copy of an early 1600s instrument that, a century later, influenced Stradivari in the development of his famed violins.

"Surprise!" his family shouted, with Alex emerging from behind a drape, Donald stepping through a doorway, and Mary advancing to offer a manual: "Violin Without a Master," its promise "to perfect the learner."

Billy was both touched and elated. Not that he'd abandon his Ophir City instrument; rather, it would reside on the parlor's mantle.

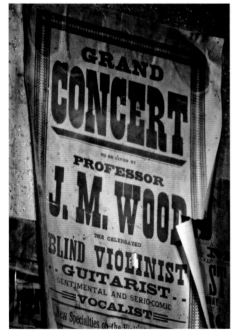

A Professor Wood broadside printed by the *Eureka Sentinel*.

In days and weeks and months ahead, he would delight in "Blasting rock by day; by night essaying a fiddle." The Gasparo da Salo's pegs didn't slip; it produced beautiful, full, rounded tones. "Sorry," he addressed his former fiddle over on the mantle; "it's not your fault that you were scratchy and given to sliding off key, as might a prospector on a boozy toot."

Billy taught himself to decipher notes and notations, to read music.

As well, Billy had a mentor, a Professor J.M. Wood, who every so often rode into town on a burro to

117

entertain Eurekans by playing his violin, strumming his guitar, singing, and offering humorous asides. He sported a walrus moustache and goggle glasses so dark Billy couldn't see his eyes. Nor could he see Billy, for he was blind. "For thirty years of peregrinations from Puget Sound to the Mexican border, I have trusted the eyesight of sure-footed quadrupeds, and never been disappointed."

"The music of birds and brooks and the perfume of flowers is compensation for what is lost to me," he told Billy, "Withal I am happy and content."

The Professor evaluated and encouraged Billy's skills, and he offered an even greater lesson: How a man seriously challenged, without a shred of self-pity, can love the desert, roam the desert, and carry on.

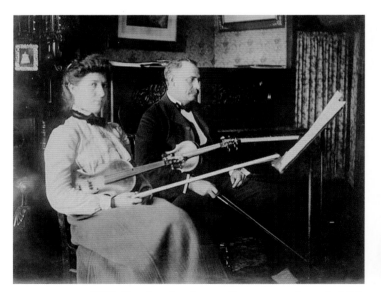 

With Eureka short on culture, parents and children were parlor guests and students.

And the time came when that there were requests that Billy teach others. He demurred at first, but then gained the confidence to accept students – on the condition that they pay no more that two bits a session.

But then, the way of the world being what it is, tragedy struck.

Up at the Ruby Hill mine, brother Alex had drilled a series of holes and packed them with dynamite, then lit a fuse, only to, *O God*, realize it was a "runner," burning faster than a man could escape. Panicked, Alex tripped and fell. Halfway to standing back up, the rock face exploded. He was blinded, blinded for life.

As had Professor J.M. Wood, he was to counter adversity with courage. He learned "finger reading," not only Braille, but four other systems as well. Indeed, when needed, he would calm Billy and offer advice as how to bow an unusual chord or master a complex run of notes.

Alexander Fraser went on to become both a County Commissioner and a State Legislator, "serving as faithfully and well the interests of his county."[23]

"Not bad, seeing as you can't see," taciturn Donald was to remark. "And you, Billy, you too appear to be making something of yourself, about time. And Mary (calling out, for she's in the kitchen), you too as well, cook and lady prospector. Why, the best such in the family."[24]

[23] C.W. Torrance, *Ibid*, chapter XIII.

[24] Mary had made and recorded as many as a dozen claims in Nevada's Esmeralda County and California's Inyo County. Their sale could have made a substantial contribution to the Frasers' welfare.

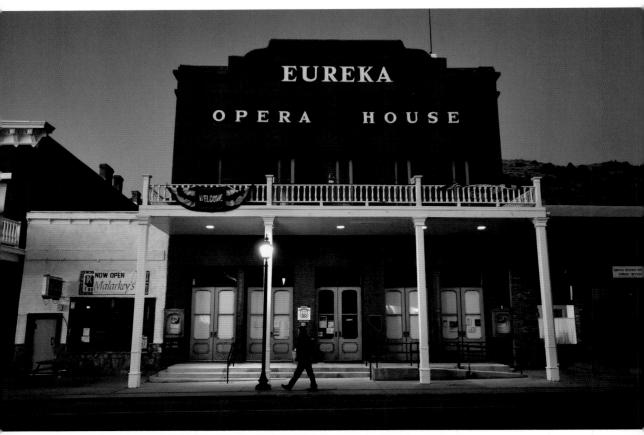

The Eureka Opera House, restored in the 21st century.

The year was now 1915, a turning point for Eureka's Opera House, one of three in Nevada, the others being Piper's in Virginia City and Thompson's in Pioche.

Donations had been solicited, and a silent movie projector purchased and shipped on the Eureka & Palisades Railroad. Not two projectors, necessary for an uninterrupted show. Just one, requiring a break after each ten-minute reel. The editor of the *Sentinel*, Eureka's long-time newspaper, carted his gramophone to the theater to provide a musical interlude. But more often than not, the crowd drawn to the old theater, packing it up to three times a week, launched into a discussion of what they'd just seen and what it meant.

The Count of Monte Cristo was a favorite (three versions 1908-1922).

In a cavern on a mysterious island, Edmond Dantes, an escaped prisoner from the dread Chateau d'If, discovers a treasure beyond belief – not that different than what Nevada miners dreamed might lay beneath their feet.

"For all he gains – gold, pearls, a floppy neckpiece, a nice enough girlfriend," asked a fellow in overalls, "isn't that enough? No, sir. The man, he wants revenge!"

Fitted with a carbide lamp and hand cranked, the Opera House's movie projector in the 1910s.

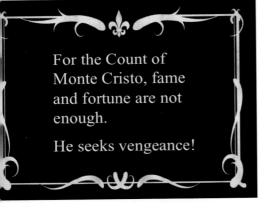

For the Count of Monte Cristo, fame and fortune are not enough.

He seeks vengeance!

"Monsieur stuck-up…"

"Pompous!"

"Self-righteous."

"You know, I'm for the other guy, the one with the little black hat."

And so forth.

The reel changed, the projector whirred on.

The Eureka Opera House was built back in 1880, the year of Billy's birth on a San Francisco dock. And the theater was inaugurated with a Nob Hill Fire Company Masquerade, which amazingly persisted as a New Year's event well into the twentieth century. Eurekans loved to dance, and with Billy's encouragement, weekly Opera House soirees were organized. To accompany waltzes, polkas, and foxtrots, Billy rustled up a quartet, two miners and two Indians. He'd play the violin, as would his friend Joe Rednui; one Shoshone, quite talented, would toot a cornet, the other would snare and thump a drum. Billy liked Indians, the ones down by the El Paso Mountains excepted.

Every Saturday night, a dance would commence at ten, and often last until dawn Sunday morning.

And every Memorial Day, the little band would march up the hill to Graveyard Flat, where they'd serenade those who'd "passed to a fair shaded land." There was a cluster of cemeteries. Catholic, Masonic, Odd Fellows, Chinese. And across the way, Jewish.

Eurekans all.

Come major holidays, the stage of the Opera House would be given to school pageants.

Otherwise, it was anyone's guess who would alight from the Eureka & Palisades train, pass out handbills and play the Opera House. Rarely, were there more than a duo or trio of entertainers, an exception being a circus consisting of "one

Eureka first-graders celebrate Washington's birthday (with George seated front-row center).

elephant, maybe Shetland ponies & monkeys. And they had dogs and, oh yes, a trapeze act."[25] If the elephant was small enough, it could have made it onto the stage. If not, Eureka offered a choice of vacant lots.

Considering Eureka's remote location, touring acts were on the sketchy side.

With the theater allegedly an "Opera House," there's the question: Was an opera ever performed there? The answer is well, no. But maybe, yes.

A " My Dear Esteemed Gentlemen" telegram came down the line, and was referred to Billy Fraser. It announced a visit by

---

[25] Old timer Albert Biale, in Robert D. McCracken, *Eureka Memories* (Eureka, Nevada: Eureka County History Project, 1994), p. 34.

Did they shoot or sing?   **Legerdemain!**   **Lightning twirls!**

𝄞 **Would he survive the rock-shattering blow?**

an opera singer, Mlle. Mignon Nevada ("Nevada" her adopted stage name). Could someone meet up with her, and show her about? Billy had heard of her. While many acts announced that they had "performed before the crowned heads of Europe," she really had. The daughter of famed soprano Emma Nevada, she, on her own, was making quite a name for herself.

And bound for Eureka!

Billy was there at the station as on schedule the Eureka & Palisades train pulled in, and a slender, even fragile looking lady alighted, roughly his same age.[26] He blurted, "Will you be performing?"

---

[26]Actually, six years younger.

She'd considered that, but no, she was here on her own, without an orchestra, costumes, or scenery.

Her reason for her detour from the main line to San Francisco was that her mother had been brought up on a ranch west of Eureka, and had spoken longingly of it, and her wish to return to her beloved Nevada. But alas, fame and fortune had set her on a different course. And so, "I'm her daughter, in her stead."

The next day, Billy arranged for a carriage, nothing fancy, to take them to the old Wixom ranch. Mignon was enchanted; her mother had described the house in detail, and her room where as a child she had lined up half dozen cigar boxes, and opened their lids, revealing the photogravure faces of Queen Victoria and Prince Albert. She would then serenade the royal couple.

On the way back, Billy again ventured the idea of a performance. "I've a band for accompaniment, and folks here aren't the least bit fussy about scenery and costumes."

He proposed a program, and the more he said, the more Mignon Nevada warmed to the idea – so much so that on their return they pulled up at the office of the *Eureka Sentinel*, to place an advertisement in the next day's paper. It promised, among other things, **"A Surprise Aria"** and the **"Triumphant March from AIDA, Performed by the Orchestra."**

As a **Grand Finale** there'd be **"In its Entirety, Act IV, of the Sensational Opera HAMLET, featuring LA SCENE FOU DE OPHELIA! OPHELIA'S MAD SCENE! Sung by Mlle. Nevada accompanied by the Orchestra under the Direction of Mr. Wm. Fraser."** The typesetter said he was sorry, but he couldn't

A star in the desert night, Mlle. Mignon Nevada.

add the accent marks that the French were fond off. "Pas de problème," smiled Mlle. Mignon.

They rehearsed the next day, Billy taking a day off from the mine, as did fellow miner Joe Rednui. The two Indians were commitment free.

The performance that night went well, in fact far better than Billy expected. The march from *Aida* was a bit of a stretch, but nobody cared as the four-piece band marched down the aisle, out into the lobby, and then triumphantly back into the theater.

Finally it was time for Ophelia's mad scene. The crowd hushed. Billy explained, "Fellow Eurekans, you must now use your imagination, and consider where I stand a lake, its depths the realm of unseen, fiery-eyed nymphs."

To welcoming applause, enter Ophelia, wrapped in garlands of flowers (picked by Eureka schoolchildren). Reclining on a sun-bleached sofa (the Act's sole prop), she sang – with heart-rending runs and agitated trills. Pale and frail, Ophelia was distraught.

Though having no idea what this was all about, the audience was moved, as Ophelia rose to erratically wander this way and that, flinging and strewing her flowers to the floor (the floor doubling as a lake).

Had anyone understood French, she was possessed by the notion of malign nymphs, luring her to a watery death.

Ophelia's reason had fled, abandoned her.

Rattling the rafters of the Opera House with her song, she fell to the floor, writhed as if drowning – and died.

The music stopped. Billy laid down his violin, and with a white shroud, covered lost-to-the-world Ophelia.

For the better part of a minute, there was a stunned silence. Then one fellow clapped, and another, and the Opera House erupted in a riot of applause, unrestrained foot-stomping, and shouts of "Mignon! Mignon! Mignon Nevada!"

Casting off her shroud, she rose. She curtsied and bowed and in a daze, curtsied again. Haunted by her role, words eluded her. She had never sung Ophelia so well. Never, anywhere.[27]

The next morning, she bid Billy goodbye, kissing him on one cheek, then the other. "Adieu" he said, and "Au revoir, chef d'orchestre," she replied as she boarded the northbound Eureka & Palisades train, on a journey that would take her on to San Francisco, then back to London's Covent Garden, the Opéra Comique in Paris, and Milan's La Scala.

As to the Frasers… after years of excitement and disappointment, it can't be said that they lived happily ever after, yet they were relatively content as the years and then the decades rolled by.

Billy had not the least regret that he'd forsaken a quest for riches (and its "gold, greed, and corruption") in favor and an enduring delight in music – his own, his student's, and the strains of footloose performers who strayed into Eureka, and played the Opera House.

---

[27] The opera *Hamlet* was composed by her godfather, French composer Ambroise Thomas. As well, he composed the popular opera *Mignon*, offering his goddaughter her first name.

For a spell, sister Mary was off to San Francisco, where in 1921 she met and married one James Wilcox. And the two of them returned to Eureka, to share the household of "Old Dad and the Kids," as they were known about town.

Donald Fraser was the first to be summoned by "sleep's pale brother" – death in a Western euphemism – and to journey to whatever lies beyond, followed by Alexander, though blind, alert and engaged until his dying day. He'd contracted silicosis back when he was able to mine gold, silver, and lead.

Billy – the Montana Kid, the Montana Outlaw, and then back to Billy again – was laid low by myocarditis, arthritis, and bronchial asthma. He was a tough old bird; it took a lot to do him in. He died on April 23, 1954, in his forty-second year in Eureka. As the end neared, his violins – both of them, for he still fiddled his homemade one – offered comfort and solace.

His last words were said to have been, "Myself, I'm pretty well wrapped up," and his last wish was that he be cremated off in Salt Lake City, with his ashes returned to Eureka, and scattered in the desert.

In sight of the Opera House, that would be nice. But in any event, nowhere near a mine.

Come night, a ghost flower.

Epilogue

In his twilight years, Billy Fraser enjoyed roaming the nearby desert's hills and valleys, to every so often be inspired by what he saw or found. Could be a coyote; could be a flower, his favorite being the ghost flower. And this would be cause for an on-the-spot sonata, bowed on whatever violin he'd taken along.

There was magic in the flower, matched by the magic of his violin.[28] It's been said, "the older the violin, the sweeter the song." And the same could be said of old Billy.

On his return to town, he'd be often heartened by the strains of another violin, its notes floating from a parlor window, the swinging doors of a saloon, or on more than one occasion, an outhouse.

For you see, he'd started something: a tradition of string-strumming Eurekans, be they bright-eyed kids or grizzly codgers – like, ultimately, himself.

---

[28]A botanist appraising Eureka's flora – possibly Sereno Watson (see footnote #1) – told Billy that the ghost flower was indeed rare, and was "on the sly side." Lacking nectar, it attracted pollen-bearing bees by its resemblance to a similar flower, the blazing star. The ghost's perpetuation then, was at the expense of duped bees. If there's a lesson in this, it could be beware the lure of all that glitters.

The time would come when Eureka would host an annual Nevada State Old Time Fiddler's Contest, drawing violinists from as far distant as Scotland. Its appeal? As an appreciative commentator mused:

> In the rapture of life, many things give meaning to the soul, like the voice within a fiddle growing stronger with each melody played. If you listen closely you may hear meanings that words will never explain.[29]

Indeed, words would never fully explain William Henry Fraser. But his homemade violin did, not only in its sweet if scratchy song accented by a bicycle bell, but in its doggerel and drawings. He aspired to be a swaggering, rank outlaw, but settled on the tamer role of a miner and weekend prospector.

Moreover, throughout the better part of his life, he was a kindly music teacher – and the fellow who brought Grand Opera to Eureka, Nevada.

Who else would have decorated his instrument with a coyote, a burro – and a rabbit?

[29]Jack Sutton of KTVN Reno's *Nevada Backroads.*

Acknowledgments

Over the years, the author has enjoyed the company of desert prospectors, miners and raconteurs Billy Blue and Bruce Minard in California, and Tommy Thompson, Martin Duffy, Lou Meyers, and Billy Varga in Nevada. In common, their gaze would shift to faraway hills, as they wondered what they might find there, and beyond. Rolled into one, they became a desert Everyman, an inspiration for the character of Billy Fraser.

Not that he's all that imagined. His wanderings are tracked in census reports, mining claims, and in two striking first-hand accounts.

Further, there is a saying that, bowed by a virtuoso, a violin sings, and courted by a fiddler, it can dance – and here we have a violin that talks, its inked poetry and images insights into Billy' Fraser's life and times – a life of apprehension and hope in a dry, desolate, yet strangely appealing land. Battered and forlorn, the instrument's modern salvation dates to a chance encounter in a windblown stall in a Mojave Desert flea market. Restoring it was a challenge, rewarded when composer-violinist Elisabeth Waldo proved it was still playable, and jauntily so, thanks to Billy's addition of a little bicycle bell.

For helpful information, thanks are due the late Beverly Kurhts, granddaughter of pioneer stage driver Jacob Kurhts. P. Gary Eller provided insights into the complex character of the poet-prospector Clarence Eddy, Linda Tandle was a genealogical whiz, Jim and Joan Price enthusiastically researched the Fraser family's stay in the environs of Goldfield, Nevada, and Chris Pyle and Molly Bosted skillfully restored period photographs.

For Sunbelt Publications, Debi Young deftly oversaw the book's production, Barry Age was its talented designer, and Rebecca Kris created its cover art. As always, Diana and Lowell Lindsay, Sunbelt's founders, offered a welcoming and appreciated hand.

At first, Bonnie, the author's wife, wasn't all that taken with crumbling camps and treacherous mines, but ultimately rather enjoyed them. "O my God, here I am looking forward to another trip to nowhere!"

Her help and good cheer was invaluable.

Back then: Nova Scotia child miners.

Finally, my life through, I've given thought to the short life of my grandfather Danny MacRae. Immigrating from Scotland to Canada at the same time as the book's Frasers,[30] he was recruited as a child miner in Stellarton, Nova Scotia's Albion workings.

He was to marry, have two children, and adopt two orphans. At the age of thirty-three he was killed by a runaway train of ore cars.

In memoriam, Daniel MacRae

[30] Indeed, the MacRaes and Frasers were closely allied clans.

Photography Credits

Multiple photographs on a page are listed clockwise from upper left (a-b-c-d).

Not listed below: photographs by author or from his collection.

i	Death Valley National Park Archives
x	National Archives
6	Bancroft Library, University of California, Berkeley
8	Bancroft Library, University of California, Berkeley
12	Huntington Library
24	Huntington Library
26	Pinterest
27	National Archives
29	Wikipedia Commons
31	Wikipedia Commons
32a	Autrey Museum of the American West
32b	WordPress
37	FotoSearch
38a	Sweet C's Design
38b	Pinterest
41	Special Collections, University of Nevada, Reno
42	Ontario Mine, Utah
43a	California State Parks
46	Stan Paher, Nevada Publications
50	Wikipedia Commons
56	Nevada State Museum
58b	Death Valley National Park Archives

59	Museum of Eastern California
60	J. Gary Eller
61	George Pipkin Collection
62	Pinterest
64	Automobile Club of Southern California
69	Automobile Club of Southern California
86	Wallpapers-Web
90	Arizona Historical Foundation
92	Nevada Historical Society
97	Bill Cox, Provo City Library, Utah
99	Central Nevada Historical Society
100	Nevada Historical Society
101	Nevada Historical Society
102	John Nevil Maskelyne, *Sharps and Flats*
103a	Nevada Historical Society
103b	John Nevil Maskelyne, *Sharps and Flats*
104	Nevada Historical Society
105	Nevada Historical Society
110	Pinterest
112	*True West Magazine*
114a	Special Collections, University of Nevada, Reno
114b	World Mining Museum, Butte
115	Special Collections, University of Nevada, Reno
118a	Etsy
120	David Becker, Alamy
122a	*The Count of Monte Cristo*, 1922
122c	*The Count of Monte Cristo*, 1922
123	Special Collections, University of Nevada, Reno
124b	iStock
124c	Harrison Putney
127	Wikipedia
134a	Pinterest
134b	iStock
134c	Library of Congress

In a cemetery overlooking Eureka, Nevada, Billy's homemade violin
rests in its coffin-like carrying case.